Surgery
Open Heart

*A Surgical Nurse Guides You
Through Open Heart Surgery:*

*From the Time You Enter the
Operating Room Until the Day
You Leave for Home*

by Steven Monteiro RN

When faced with the challenges of life: turn to them, confront them, and know that your inner strength and fortitude can conquer all ...

purposes solely and is universal as so. The presentation of the information is without contract or any type of guarantee assurance. The information offered is not the rendering of any medical or professional advice. All information offered in this book is offered only as suggestions and is not to be intended as any type of substitute for actual medical advice from a physician.

As with any medical or surgical procedure, results will vary among individuals, and there could be substantial risks involved. All concerns should be discussed with your medical doctor and his/her associate healthcare providers prior to any treatment or surgery. As with any medical procedure informed consent, along with working knowledge of said procedure, must be established before execution. The information presented in this book about heart surgery and all its associated outcomes is offered for educational purposes only. Do not act or rely upon this information without seeking independent professional medical advice from a licensed medical doctor. **In all circumstances, either informational or physical or conceptual, your doctor's advice takes total precedence over any information offered in this book. Do not act on or use any of the information presented in this book over the advice of your own medical doctor or his/her associated healthcare professionals.** The transmission of this information does not create any relationship between you and the author or any co-authors associated with this book. The author or co-author does not guarantee the accuracy, completeness, usefulness, or adequacy of any information available at or from this transmission. The author or co-author shall not be responsible or liable for any loss or damages resulting from the informational suggestions found in this book.

The authors do not assume any responsibility for errors or lack of accuracy in content at any third-party websites or other publications offered in these writings. The authors of this book do not guarantee any medical advice offered at any third-party websites or publications suggested within this book.

The trademarks that are used are without any consent, and the publication of the trademark is without permission or backing by the trademark owner. All trademarks and brands within this book are for clarifying purposes only and are owned by the owners themselves, not affiliated with this document.

Table of Contents

Acknowledgements:

Special thanks to Jessica Meyer RN for her insight and help with this book.

Preface

Thank you for purchasing the book *Surgery Open Heart: A Surgical Nurse Guides You Through Open Heart Surgery—From the Time You Enter the Operating Room Until the Day You Leave for Home.* Congratulations on taking an active role in your heart surgery process. Several different people will care for you during your stay in the hospital. Some of them you will see on a regular basis, while others you may not remember because you will be under anesthesia when they care for you. There will be some you will never see because they care for you by monitoring your vital signs and your health records from remote parts of the hospital. However, all of us as healthcare professionals inherently know that the more you are aware of the process, the more comfortable and profitable your journey will be. Moreover, statistically speaking, the more comfort and knowledge you possess, the better your outcome.

Just visiting the doctor's office for a checkup can be scary. *What was my blood pressure? Is that good or bad?* There are so many things to worry about! Open heart surgery creates a lot more questions, new stressors, and big words that are as scary as the word "cancer." This book is written for the open heart surgery patient and his/her family members who are not familiar with the medical field but who suddenly find themselves immersed in the foreign medical world of tests, procedures, and interventions.

This book is generalized for all open heart surgery patients. Definitions of words are explained as they are used in the hope of making them just a bit less frightening. Your caregivers and doctors can give you further details about your particular case. There are benefits and risks for every surgery, especially one as important as heart surgery. Following the current guidelines in this book and from your hospital caregivers may help minimize your risks and lead you to a positive surgical outcome.

Thanks again for purchasing this book. I hope you enjoy it and that it helps you or your loved one get through open heart surgery

Introduction

Okay, let's say it and get it over with — surgery is scary! It is probably one of the most frightening experiences we have to face in life. So, the question must be brought forth and answered: *Why is it so scary?*

First, it is an unknown. Most people can age well into their 60's and never see the inside of an operating room. They have no idea what the room is going to feel or look like, or what's going to happen to them once they are inside. For others, it is the pain. Some people hate needles and injections; they worry about post-op pain. However, don't forget that we as healthcare providers have an arsenal of drugs and techniques that significantly limit the amount of pain one must endure in this modern medical age.

Then there is the giving up of control. Once you are placed on the stretcher to be wheeled into the O.R., you have given up all control to your caregivers. You must trust that they know what they are doing and that they have your best interests in mind — which, by the way, they do. And then, of course, there is the mortality issue: "*Am I going to make it through this operation? Is something going to go wrong? Am I going to die?*"

The answer to your last question is a resounding ... NO!

At least statistically you are not. The mortality rate for open heart surgeries in some clinics/hospitals is on average about two percent. That means you will probably be in much more danger driving to the hospital than you will be as a surgical patient within the hospital.

Having said all that, let's prepare you for your surgery. Let's go step by step. Let's identify all the players and their roles, and all the procedures you may encounter. Let's get you into the O.R. so that we can start your journey of recovery and safely return you to your life at home.

Chapter 1: Diagnosis, Pre-Tests, and Preparation

By now you have seen (or will soon see) a cardiologist and have been diagnosed with some form of heart disease:

- Mitral Valve Stenosis

- Aortic Valve Stenosis

- Tricuspid Valve Stenosis

- Coronary Artery Disease

- Atrial/Ventricular Septal Defect

- Aortic Aneurysm

- Atrial Fibrillation

- Atrial Myxoma

You have gone through a battery of pre-op tests:

- **Echocardiogram:** Although there are several versions of this test (stress echo, doppler echo, transthoracic echo), it was performed so that the doctor could see how the blood flowed through your heart. Your doctor was also seeing whether your heart is enlarged, how your valves are working, or whether there are any clots or tumors within your heart.

- **CT Scan:** This *Cardiac Computerized Tomography* test is essentially an x-ray of your heart. With the aid of a computer, this test combines several x-ray images to produce a cross section of your heart. This test could be performed either with or without IV contrast dye. Just like the echocardiogram has several versions, so does this test.

- **MRI (Magnetic Resonance Imaging):** If you had this test, you were definitely asked a million times whether you had any metal with you or inside you. The magnet in a typical MRI is 30,000 times stronger than the earth's magnetic field. It has been known to grab four-foot metal oxygen tanks and turn them into flying missiles. This test creates moving pictures (as well as still images) of your heart and its major blood vessels.

- **EKG (Electrocardiogram):** This would have been one of your earlier tests, a 12-lead EKG. This non-invasive test tells your doctor about the electrical energy of your heart — whether your heart is too slow (bradycardia) or too fast (tachycardia). It can even indicate whether you had a silent heart attack in the past.

- **H & P (History and Physical):** Even if you are having very minor surgery, most doctors will insist that you go to your primary care doctor and get a complete physical prior to surgery. This is done to ensure that your health is good enough to allow for anesthesia and your upcoming surgery.

- **Blood Tests:** You were definitely asked to visit a lab and have your blood drawn for testing. The tests were most likely: a CBC (complete blood count) to measure the type of blood cells you have, whether you have an infection or whether you are anemic; Chem. 7, which, among other things, checks your kidney functions; and a liver functional panel, which checks how well your liver is working.

- **Pulmonary Function Tests:** The surgery is on your heart, but your lungs are very important for getting you through surgery! Pulmonary function tests (PFTs) can show how well your lungs are working before surgery.

- **Exercise Stress Test:** This test is sometimes referred to as the *treadmill test*. This test will show the physician how your heart reacts to exertion. The patient walks on a treadmill with increasing speed and incline; his/her EKG, heart rate, blood pressure, and respiratory rate are measured during and immediately after this exercise stress. This test can determine at what point your heart rhythm may change or when your heart becomes ischemic (decreased blood flow to the heart muscle), possibly causing angina (chest pain). This test, like the tests listed previously, also has many variances: the echo stress test, nuclear/thallium stress test, and dobutamine stress test, to name just a few.

- **Coronary Angiogram:** This test would most likely have been done after all the other non-invasive tests were completed. This test is an invasive test in that it involves a catheter entering your body, either through your groin (femoral artery) or most likely through your wrist (radial artery). An interventional cardiologist would have passed a catheter into your heart and have taken x-rays (angiograms) of your heart vessels while injecting a radiopaque dye. By looking at these films he/she and your surgeon can determine where blockages exist on your heart. If coronary artery bypass is determined to be necessary, your surgeon

5

will use these films to accurately bypass the blockages. If your interventional cardiologist sees an obstruction that he/she can access and stent (and that this stenting negates an open heart operation), he/she may fix the blockage right there and then while you are on the table. This procedure is done with a local anesthetic while you are completely awake or mildly sedated.

Funny Story:

I once had a patient whose primary language was not English; to compound this issue, he was also frightened of needles. He went to the lab with his son for a blood draw for pre-surgical lab tests. Because of his fear of needles, he thought it would be okay to have his son get the blood drawn for him. Obliging, the son rolled up his sleeve, went into the office and got his blood drawn for his dad. To compound matters, they both had the same name, with the son being a "Junior." How we caught this one the day of surgery was amazing, but through our many checks and balances we did catch it; his surgery was canceled that day and he was sent to the lab for his own blood draw!

Most large hospitals have a PATC (pre-admission testing center) that takes care of all your medical tests in one facility. This is ideal for you as a patient in that all your tests can be done at one place, usually all in one day.

Along with all the tests listed, your surgeon and his surgical team will perform a physical exam and take a medical history. Be honest about your allergies, medications, past medical conditions, previous surgeries, drug use, alcohol use, smoking frequency, and family history. Taking a family member who is close to you can help your surgical team identify risk factors that may cause complications during surgery. You want to be as healthy as possible before surgery so you can recover quickly and smoothly. Now is a perfect time to quit smoking and start eating healthily. This way you will be ready for surgery and in excellent health after your surgery is complete. The healthier your body is before surgery, the better your outcome may be.

How Do I Pick the Best Surgeon?

Once your cardiologist has determined that you need heart surgery, his/her next step is to refer you to a heart surgeon for a surgical consult. Most would think that this is a straightforward process and, of course, the cardiologist has your best interests in mind, *right?* So, the cardiologist will naturally pick the best cardiac surgeon available. However, if there is one cardiac surgeon who is considered the best, every single cardiologist cannot always pick him; there are just too many patients for that to occur.

This process varies from hospital to hospital. Some hospitals have strict protocols, and the cardiologist simply picks whichever surgeon is up next on a rotating list. However, in reality, most cardiologists have working relationships with certain surgeons and it is those surgeons they would recommend on a regular basis.

In other words, every cardiologist has his/her favorite surgeon to whom he/she sends most referrals.

Plus, not every cardiac surgeon performs all types of heart surgeries. For example, not every heart surgeon performs heart transplants. Some may specialize in valve surgery, while others do only bypass surgery. This differs not only from surgeon to surgeon but from institution to institution, with variances across the country.

However, remember this: You are not under any obligation to use the cardiologist's recommendation for a surgeon. You are free to search for and find someone on

7

your own, anywhere in the country. Just keep in mind that not every surgeon or institution may fall within your insurance limitations.

A patient on a heart forum I follow wrote the following about finding a surgeon to repair his heart valve:

"From what I've read experience is very important when it comes to repairs... I didn't go with the first surgeon I was assigned; he was highly rated, but I pushed for the guy who trained him. When I asked to switch, my cardiologist seemed to imply I was asking a bit much. The surgeon I went with does, on average, over 200 OHS [open heart surgeries] a year and specializes in repairs, so I assumed they make up a good percentage of his surgeries. He's been using a technique he helped develop since 2004 so going by rudimentary math that's...um...a hell of a lot. More important to me was the fact he has no re-ops due to valve failure over that 11-[year] period. I only wanted repair if it's likely to last. I was 45 when I had my surgery, and my backup choice was mechanical."

The American Heart Association recommends the grassroots method of finding a doctor/surgeon: *good old-fashioned word of mouth.* Family, friends and former patients are always good sources of information. However, be sure to take it further and make sure your doctor is affiliated with reputable institutions. Also, be certain that your surgeon has performed a significant number of your type of procedure and that his rate of complications is low. The average cardiac surgeon statistically performs around 120 surgeries a year. Don't be afraid to ask the hard questions. Many patients are intimidated by doctors and tend to take a subservient role when dealing with them. However, when the situation is stripped of all its pomp and circumstance, you are hiring and paying this person to heal you. It is in your best interest to vet him/her as you would when hiring any other person to work for you. Don't be afraid to ask his mortality rate. This may be a hard subject to broach, but it is your life we are talking about. His mortality rate should be very low, less than 2 percent and his complication rate less than 8 percent.

However, even as I write this I am reminded of an excellent heart surgeon I use to work with that was always approached to do the most complicated cases — the cases other surgeons refused to do because they were deemed too risky and complex. If left unattended, these patients would certainly succumb to their disease. Throughout his career, he probably saved the lives of hundreds of patients that would otherwise not have received a heart operation. However, I am confident it skewed his mortality and morbidity rate; so in rankings he didn't look as competent as his great skills warranted.

The bottom line is that you must feel comfortable with your surgeon. When you are with the surgeon, does he offer hope and comfort, or is his personality off-putting? Are you both on the same page when it comes to the course of treatment he is offering you? A good practice to follow is to bring along a family member or friend who can listen to the conversation you have with your surgeon. This trusted person can then offer you an objective view and advice.

A good barometer for vetting a surgeon for any type of specialty is whether his/her colleagues (anesthesiologist, nurses, and techs) have previously asked him/her to operate on themselves or their family members. In every hospital the staff and colleagues of a surgeon know who is best. Some surgeons are constantly asked to see the loved ones of colleagues, *while some surgeons are never asked...*

Your Surgical Approach

Once you find and sit down with your chosen surgeon, the two of you will discuss, among many things, your surgical approach. This will be how your surgeon gains access to your heart and your given heart ailment. His/her access, logically, will depend on your heart problem: aortic valve disease, mitral valve disease, coronary artery disease, or an aortic aneurysm, to name just a few. There are basically three main approaches to your chest when performing heart surgery.

1. **Full Sternotomy:** This approach (also called a Median Sternotomy) is the most widely accepted access for most types of heart surgery. With this approach, your surgeon makes a six to eight-inch incision in your chest and through your entire sternum. (Your sternum, or breastbone, is the hard bone you feel in the center of your chest.) He then uses a retractor to spread your chest apart, giving him full access to your entire heart, aorta, and other major vessels. It is the easiest and fastest way for your surgeon to perform your operation.

2. **Mini Sternotomy:** In this approach, your eight-inch sternal incision is reduced to about three to five inches. This method is used mainly for valve replacements. If it is a three-inch upper sternal incision, it is most likely for an aortic valve replacement. A lower short incision would probably be done for a mitral valve replacement. One might assume that these approaches are for cosmetic reasons only; however, as you will learn later in this book, it is the healing of your sternum that is one of the most debilitating parts of your recovery. Limiting the amount of sternum cut will

significantly increase your recovery time post-operatively.

In most cases, this approach does warrant an extra incision. In order to place you on the heart-lung machine (the machine that circulates and oxygenates your blood), your surgeon will most likely have to access an artery or vein in your groin. In a full sternotomy, your surgeon has enough space to access your venous and arterial systems right there in your chest. This becomes important only in that you are more susceptible to infections in your groin area and it is another place where you could develop post-op bleeding. This approach also means that in most cases you will have a longer operation and will be on the heart-lung machine much longer.

3. **Minimally Invasive Heart Surgery:** With this approach, your sternum is left completely intact. Your surgeon gains access to your heart by making small incisions on the side of your chest between the ribs, just below your armpits and toward the front of your body. Surgeons refer to this approach as *sternum-sparing*. Conversely, as is the case with the mini-sternotomy, you will most likely have other places (either your groin or your armpit area) where your surgeon will need to access your venous or arterial system.

Through this approach, your surgeon can perform many of the types of surgeries offered by a full sternotomy: coronary artery bypass, mitral and aortic valve replacement, myxomas and intracardiac tumor removals.

Under this category, you may hear the following terms:

11

- **Midcab (Minimally Invasive Direct Coronary Artery Bypass):** Here your surgeon performs coronary artery bypass through a small incision between your ribs. This approach is usually best when the patient needs only one to three bypasses on the front of the heart.

- **Robotic Assisted:** In this type of surgery, your surgeon will make several small incisions into your chest wall between the ribs. However, instead of needing to make the incision large enough to get his hands into your chest, he needs to make the incisions only large enough to place tiny robotic surgical instruments. Your surgeon sits at a console, much like a video game, and controls the movements of the robotic arms. Depending on your surgeon's skills, he/she may be able to do robotic coronary artery bypass, valve replacement, myxoma removal, ablation, atrial septal defect, or even foramen ovale repair (a hole in your heart).

- **Port Access/Limited Access/Mini Thoracotomy:** These are other terms you may hear; they are verbal variances of the above approaches.

Okay, so where are we going with all this? I'm so glad you asked.

The surgical approach your surgeon uses has a direct effect on the quality of your recovery. A minimally invasive approach may take hours longer than the traditional median sternotomy; however, the benefits may vastly outweigh the risks of a longer procedure. For although a full sternotomy provides excellent access to the heart, the resulting wound requires several months to heal completely. This significantly extends your recovery and seriously restricts your post-op activity for *months!*

Here is a list of some of the benefits of a modified *(sternal sparing)* incision:

- Smaller incisions and smaller scars.

- Decreased post-op physical limitations. When you do not cut through the breastbone, your recovery can go from six to eight weeks to less than four weeks. *The sternum takes a very long time to heal.*

- Decreased hospital stay. Some patients with minimally invasive surgery leave the hospital in three to five days, while the traditional heart patient can be hospitalized for five or more days.

- No risk of sternal infections. If your surgeon does not have to cut through your sternum, the potential for a sternal infection is most likely zero. Your sternum is a very large bone, and sternal wound infections are severe and debilitating.

- Less post-op surgical pain. A small incision on the side of your chest is considerably less painful than an incision through the center of your sternum.

- Women with osteoporosis are at a greater risk for complications when it comes to bone healing, especially the sternum. A sternal-sparing incision for this population may be a great compromise. Also, cosmetically, women can wear low-cut necklines without revealing any scars.

- No worry about sternal precautions. *This is a big one.* As you read further into this book, you will come to realize that the major incapacitating process of this entire operation is your sternal incision. For weeks on end, you will not be allowed to pick up anything heavier than 10 pounds. *And let's not even talk about sneezing.* I address that further on in the book.

The Night Before

Once you have chosen your surgeon, done all your pre-tests, spent several nights worrying and ruminating...eventually comes the night before surgery. Are you ready mentally and physically? Some patients are prepared. They come to surgery ready to conquer this mountain. Others say to me, *"I just want to get this over with." Which ones do you think do better?*

Being nervous or even scared is normal. Some people fear the pain, some waking up with an endotracheal tube in their throat; others fear whether their heart can take the strain. But you must hold on to the statistics, which state that up to 97 percent of heart surgery patients do just fine!

Here is the anxiety and triumph journey of one of our *Surgery Open Heart Facebook* members, Halee:

Hello, I am new to the page! I am 24 years old and will undergo OHS this Thursday, December 1st. I have done a lot of research but the more, the better, right! So if anyone has any advice on what they would have done differently or just a little bit about what it's like waking up from surgery with the breathing tube! I am very nervous about that part; I feel like I will "freak out." Any advice about how soon to get up and walk, medications, things I should and shouldn't do. Things to bring to the hospital. Also how long was your stay in ICU and in the hospital in general? Thanks!

So tomorrow's the big day!!! OHS will be about 11-12 lunch time! I have been in high spirits all day; now it's late at night, and it's kind of starting to hit me! But I know God has a plan, and all will be great! Wish my surgical team luck and for me for a speedy recover. It would be greatly appreciated!!!

So for an update for those who are wondering! Everything is going great! I actually was in ICU that whole night and the next day I went to the step-down unit! I actually went home on day three post-OHS in the hospital; everyone was shocked about it. But I felt good; the pain meds were working, the incision looked great, as well as the heart. So the doctors sent me home. Which I was glad about. My chest tubes came out the day after surgery because after x-rays and up and walking, the drainage stopped. I was very happy about that! Overall my experience has had its ups and downs and overall [was] not as bad as I thought. I know that sounds silly, but that's exactly how I feel. I believe what helped me the most dealing with the pain and discomfort was the mindset going into it! I told myself, yes it's going to hurt, but we can do it and get over this hill. All the prayers and family has helped tremendously as well!! Thanks, everyone so much!

It should be noted that Halee's young age and excellent physical condition were most likely significant contributors to her astonishingly fast recovery. She had an ASD and VSD repair. *Halee, thanks for allowing me to share your journey!*

Either directly or through his/her nurse, your surgeon would have instructed you regarding what medications to take (and not take) before surgery. The drugs that are a major concern before surgery are the blood thinners: aspirin, Coumadin, Plavix, and others. These medications can cause excessive bleeding and could prolong or jeopardize your operation. However, always follow your doctor's orders; some blood thinners may not be stopped before your procedure, and your doctor would be keenly aware of such situations.

If you are experiencing any severe cold-like symptoms one to three days before your surgery, be sure to let your surgeon's office know. The flu or severe congestion may warrant the cancellation of your surgery. Breathing deeply and comfortably after surgery is a big concern for everyone, and severe congestion could compromise your surgical results and even put you on the road to pneumonia.

Most heart surgeons schedule one or two heart operations a day; the faster ones will schedule three. If you are given the choice of first or second, *always take the first!* You may have to wake up much earlier, but it will be well worth it. There are so many variables in a surgeon's day that if you take the second slot, you are at risk of several occurrences that arise all the time.

The first surgery may become complicated, delaying your start time by hours. I have seen second cases delayed by more than six hours. And if you thought you were hungry after eight hours of no food, try adding six hours to that ordeal. Also, in consideration of your family waiting with you, try to avoid this for their benefit. I have seen emergency hearts come up from the E.R. or cath lab, bumping your surgery completely — sending you back home or to be admitted to the floor for surgery the following day.

If any medications are to be taken, your doctor will most likely advise that you use only enough water to swallow the pills (a sip) — no more. It is imperative that you not have anything to eat or drink the night before surgery. Double-check your NPO time (the last time you can eat or drink the night before surgery) and whether it is okay to have sips of water to take your medications. You may be instructed to continue your medications like normal up until you report for surgery, or you may be told to stop certain medications for a few days before your surgical date. Understand any changes that must be made to your medications. And don't forget about vitamins and herbs; your surgeon or his caregiver would have discussed these beforehand. Remember that many herbs and vitamins can be considered medicinal in nature.

Along with your medication instructions, you would have received instructions on showering and cleanliness. *Nothing ruins a good operation like a surgical wound infection.* One of the most common reasons people return to the hospital after an operation, or are delayed in leaving the hospital is surgical wound infection. This is why you will be given very specific showering tasks one to five days before your operation. **Don't ignore or curtail these instructions.**

This is because one of the primary sources of these wound infections is right now living on your skin. Now don't freak out, but your body is teeming with billions of bacteria! When kept where they belong, these bacteria (natural flora) actually benefit us humans and keep us healthy. However, when deposited where they do not belong, for example— inside a surgical incision, they can wreak havoc.

It is because of these bacteria that your surgeon will ask you to shower using, most likely, chlorhexidine gluconate (Hibiclens) or a similar antibacterial-type soap. The lower you can get the number of skin bacteria on the body, the safer your surgical procedure will be. Be sure you follow his instructions precisely. This will mo using fresh towels and freshly washed be before. Every hospital has variant proced same hoped-for positive outcomes.

If you have hair on your chest or groin/leg areas, you will most likely be told not to shave yourself. Some well-meaning patients will shave their surgical area themselves, thinking it will help the surgical staff. Some do so out of modesty and can't imagine having someone shave their private areas for them. However, when your hair is cut, it can irritate the hair follicles and cause skin abrasions. These microscopic nicks provide a favorable place for bacteria to colonize, the result being a post-op wound infection. Today's modern hospitals no longer use razors that can nick the skin. An electric hair clipper will be utilized instead.

Shampoo your hair and shower according to your doctor's orders the night before surgery. Follow all directions for pre-op cleansing and skip using lotions, creams, or other powders on your skin. This will ensure that the prep solution the surgeon uses before making his incision is directly on your skin and able to work properly. Try to relax and enjoy this shower. It may be the last shower you have for at least a week. You get daily bed baths after surgery, but it is just not the same as your own shower. By the end of their hospital stays, most patients say they cannot wait to get home and take a shower!

It sometimes helps to pack a small bag of essentials you can take with you to the hospital. The hospital will provide toiletries, but if you truly like your own brand of toothpaste and toothbrush, bring them along. Bring something you can use during your stay to keep your mind off the boredom of being stuck in the hospital — crossword puzzles, magazines, a book, or cards. Bring glasses, hearing aids, canes, walkers, or anything else you use daily. Many patients recommend bringing slip-on shoes. Bending over to tie your shoes will be nearly impossible post-operatively. If you do buy slip-on shoes be sure they have good grips on their soles; hospital floors are smooth and your walks will be unsteady at best.

As you heal during your hospital stay, you will change rooms several times. You will see the operating room, the intensive care unit, and the inpatient ward. You may take road trips to radiology for follow-up tests. Leave jewelry and valuables at home or with a family member so that they are not lost as you move throughout the hospital. If you wear adult pads, are having your menstrual cycle, or have any other bodily functions that may embarrass you, don't worry about it. You are among professionals. We see it all and will always respect and honor your dignity.

Sweet dreams! Sleep well! Tomorrow's the big day!

Chapter 2: The Surgical Day

Most hospitals are like airports — we like to get you in really early and then have you wait! It is not unusual to arrive at the hospital by 5:00 a.m. and not be wheeled to the O.R. until 7:30 a.m. However, you will be experiencing a flurry of activity during that time.

Before I tell you about the first person you will meet and the people after that, let me tell you whom you will most likely not see that day. I have, from time to time, had patients ask me when they were going to see their cardiologist. For many patients, this is someone they have come to know and trust. The cardiologist's presence would certainly offer them solace. However, it would be extremely rare for your cardiologist to be there on your surgical day. Moreover, with very few exceptions, the cardiologist is never in the O.R. So, having said that, let's get you admitted and on your way.

The first person you will most likely meet the day of your operation is the admissions coordinator. This person's task is to record all the following: date of birth, full name, address, and, of course, insurance. *Don't forget your I.D. and insurance card!* They will print out the ever-present wristband that every patient must wear. They will also have you look at it to be sure all the information on it is correct. This will include your full name and your date of birth. It will also have your newly formed medical record number, as well as a hospital number. Once you are checked in, an aide will escort you to the pre-op area, where you will most likely meet your first nurse. However, before we talk to this person, let's take a look at who is accompanying you...

It is rare for a patient to arrive for surgery without a friend or family member with them. Most have immediate family members or close friends in tow. Be sure to find out the hospital's policy on how many people can accompany you. Some hospitals will allow only one, maybe two, family members in the pre-op area with you. I have seen patients arrive with an entourage of people only to have most them sent to another floor to sit for hours even before the patient is wheeled to the operating room. Moreover, if you have not heard about HIPAA (Health Insurance Portability and Accountability Act), you may encounter it if you are not an immediate family member and are waiting for information and results about a loved one. One of HIPAA's goals is to protect the confidentiality and security of healthcare information — your healthcare information, to be precise. What that means for most people is that the hospital will not reveal anything about a patient's status unless you are an immediate family member.

Where's my wife?!

If you browse the Internet, you will find several crazy stories about patient and family frustrations with the HIPAA laws. I know of a story that took place at a hospital, where a husband dropped off his wife at the front so that she wouldn't have to walk all the way from the parking lot. She checked in at the front desk and was told where to go. After parking the car and walking to the hospital, the husband went to the front desk, told them he had dropped off his wife to be admitted, and wanted to meet up with her now. He was promptly told that because of HIPAA laws, the hospital could not confirm or deny whether his wife was admitted or, if she was, where she could be found!

Your pre-op nurse will get you settled in with a change of clothes. And, yes, hospitals still use the cloth or paper

21

"johnnies" that never seem to close in the back and that no patient can ever figure out how to put on! However, most hospital gowns now have a new device called a *"Bair Hugger."* This device blows warm air into your gown; it is a wonderful feeling. It not only warms you, but the sound and the air have a very relaxing effect.

Your Pre-Op Nurse Interview

Next, a nurse's aide will come by and take your vital signs: blood pressure, temperature, and weight. In most hospitals, this is done by the aide and not the nurse, so if you have medical questions, be patient and ask the nurse and not the aide. When the nurse comes by, she will introduce herself and try to make you comfortable. Once you settle in, she will interview you and ask a myriad of questions. I will outline the most common ones and the reasons behind them:

- **What is your full name and date of birth?** This is for obvious reasons. She will be sure that all the numbers on your wrist tag match your chart and your responses, and that you are you. *You would be surprised how many people try to sneak in for free heart surgery!*

- **When was the last time you had anything to eat or drink?** You will soon find out that this is going to be the question of the day. Not eating or drinking prior to surgery is crucial for your airway safety! More details about this will be explained later.

- **Do you have any allergies to medications, food, or Latex?** This will be explained in depth later in this book, so hang in there, please.

- **What is your operation today and who is your surgeon?** When I ask this question, it is always prefaced with, "Everything I ask you, I know the answer to, I must ask just to double check." Even with this preface, you would be surprised at how many patients gasp and say, "You don't know?" We do, of course, know. These are all checks and balances to ensure your safety.

- **Do you have any metal in your body: pacemakers, hip screws, metal plates?** This question is asked mainly because one of the machines used in the operating room, called a Bovie, is used to cauterize bleeders in your tissue as the surgeon operates. In its simplest explanation, a sticky pad is placed on you so that it can be attached to the Bovie machine. The doctor wants this pad set away from any metal that can interfere with its operation.

- **What medications are you on and what did you take this morning?** Bring a list of medicines you are on. This is very helpful, especially if your medications are plenty.

Along with this interview, your nurse will be checking your chart for H&P (the history and physical done by your primary doctor). He/she will also check that all your tests are in your chart; that would be all your x-rays, diagnostics, and blood tests. Once all this is accomplished, the nurse will start an IV ("intravenous" is a term that means "into the vein"). This IV can be in either your hand or your arm. It is a sharp needle, so it hurts a bit, but please try and stay still so that it can be inserted smoothly. The needle is removed, and a small straw-like tube (catheter) remains in the vein to allow you to receive medications that work quickly in the bloodstream. The pain is temporary and once the needle is removed and the catheter left in, there is no more pain.

This will be the first of 4 IV's you will most likely receive. But don't worry — the first two are usually in the pre-op area when you are awake. The remainder should occur after you're asleep. Yay!

Think of an IV as a direct line to your body. It is the most important avenue for the administration of drugs. In every emergency, one of the first tasks attempted is IV access; without this, necessary medication cannot be delivered. Your new IV will be hooked to a bag of IV fluid, usually Lactated Ringer or Normal Saline. These fluids or crystalloid solutions have similar properties to your body and cells.

What's that you just put in my nose?

Today's hospitals are becoming very aggressive in their battle against *HAIs* (hospital/healthcare-associated infections). These are infections that patients would not normally acquire if they were not physically in a hospital setting. These infections come directly from hospital-related interventions: catheters, breathing tubes, IV's, incisions, and contact with other patients and hospital personnel. A hospital-associated infection comes with high risks and can cause complications that result in significant patient illness and a prolonged hospital stay.

One of the main culprits of these infections is *Staphylococcus aureus* (more commonly known as MRSA). MRSA is a very prevalent and resistant bacterium that has plagued hospitals for decades. *Staph aureus* is the leading cause of surgical site infections and the main reservoir of this bacteria comes from people themselves; up to 50 percent of healthy adults are colonized with this strain – *and guess where they like to colonize?*

That's right, your nose! Nearly 80 percent of patients who experience surgical-site infections have S aureus in their nasal passages.

Studies have shown that swabbing a patient's nose with an antiseptic (povidone iodine, betadine solution) or an antibiotic (mupirocin) can result in the destruction of 99.5 percent of the *S aureus* found in their nasal passages — hopefully warding off a wound infection. So while you are in the pre-op area, don't be surprised if someone comes by and paints the inside of your nose brown with betadine!

Your Anesthesia Interview

This next interview will vary from hospital to hospital, but an anesthesiologist, anesthesia resident, physician assistant (PA) anesthesia nurse, or certified registered nurse anesthetist (CRNA) will conduct this interview.

They all work for the anesthesia department, and each can complete this interview and any line placements that will soon be performed. However, before they ask you all the same questions you just answered, let's see if I can separate and define their roles for you.

- **Anesthesiologist:** Out of everyone on the list, this is the only one who is an M.D. (medical doctor). He will be the one in charge of your anesthesia care. The anesthesiologist will have the final word as to all your anesthesia decisions. He also has the authority, even over your surgeon, to cancel your case if for any reason he decides that it should not be performed. Over the years, I have seen anesthesiologists cancel a myriad of surgical cases. This is done for many reasons; however, usually it is because the anesthesiologist does not feel that the patient is medically sound enough to handle the operation. Please don't think of this as a negative. The anesthesiologist has your best interests in mind. Think of him as a *final safety net*. His job is to get you safely through the operation, and if the anesthesiologist feels that at this point in time you are not strong enough to do so, he will cancel your surgery!

- **Anesthesia Residents:** These are medical doctors who have graduated from medical school and are now training in a particular field. In this case, their field of choice is anesthesiology. In three to four years they will become attending anesthesiologists.

- **P.A. (Physician Assistant):** By now most people have been exposed to and know the role of P.A.'s. These healthcare workers work directly under a doctor and are licensed to complete many of the procedures and perform many of the functions of a physician. They can write prescriptions, conduct medical exams, order medical tests, and assist in surgery, all under the direct care of a physician.

- **CRNA (Certified Registered Nurse Anesthetist):** A CRNA is a nurse who has taken the extra step of becoming an anesthetist. This discipline is a master's degree study in anesthesia. He or she can perform most of the anesthesia administration that the anesthesiologist does. You will probably find that, in most surgical arenas, it is a nurse anesthetist who is the one taking care of you during your surgery. They work directly under the anesthesiologist and can take care of their patients just as competently as an anesthesiologist.

- **Anesthesia Nurse:** This is an RN who works for the anesthesia department. He or she is not to be confused with the CRNA. They function as a nurse only. They just happen to work for the anesthesia department, no different from the surgical nurse who works for the operating room department.

Now they are going to ask the same questions your pre-op nurse just asked, so be patient; however, their questioning will quickly become more in-depth. The ultimate goal of all these inquiries is to assess your medical conditions in order to reduce any seen or unseen problems that may arise during your surgery. They will perform a thorough patient history, assessing your present illness as well as your past illnesses. They will evaluate your medical history: hypertension, liver or kidney disease, diabetes, strokes, infections — the list is thorough, if not endless. They will want to know what medications you are on and what you have taken the night before and the day of your surgery. I have had many patients worry that they have not taken a particular medicine the day of their surgery (i.e., their blood pressure or diabetes medication). Don't fret, as there is not a single medication you may need that the hospital does not possess.

They will also want to know your history with anesthesia, if any. Your history report will help them determine what type of anesthesia is best for you. Examples of these questions may be whether you have had nausea or vomiting from past anesthesia encounters. They will also ask about your social history (alcohol consumption, tobacco use, illicit drugs). Be honest; they are not there to judge you and, believe me, we have heard it all. Your family medical and anesthesia history will be assessed, i.e., "Have any family members had difficulties with anesthesia?" And, yes, genetic history does affect your surgical and anesthesia experience. Some of these questions can get very personal and in depth. If you have friends or family members with you and you want to keep your health history private, now would be a good time to ask them to step out of the room.

I would be remiss as a nurse if I did not mention a rare inherited life-threatening condition called **Malignant Hyperthermia**. This condition is usually triggered when a genetically susceptible person is exposed to some anesthesia gasses and drugs. It usually occurs in males and adults under the age of 30. Its incidence is varied in literature, but one in 100,000 seems to be the average occurrence. Malignant hyperthermia is inherited; only one parent has to carry the gene to pass it on to a child. If you have a family history of uncles, aunts, or cousins having a profound crisis during anesthesia or surgery, please keep this in mind. Again, it is extremely rare, and every anesthesiologist is trained in recognizing and treating this rare occurrence. In my 30-plus years in the operating room, I have seen it occur only twice. If you even think that you might be one of these patients, mention it to your doctor early. There are modern, non-invasive tests that can determine if you are susceptible. If you are, it is very easy for your anesthesiologist to avoid the particular drugs and gasses that trigger a reaction.

Many years ago, we had a medical student come to the O.R. to observe an operation. He had ambitions of being a doctor and maybe working in the O.R. In casual conversation, this medical student mentioned that there was a history of M.H. (Malignant Hyperthermia) in his family. The anesthesiologist he was talking to reluctantly but immediately told him he could not stay in the O.R. The possibility of seeping anesthetic gasses posed too much of a risk for this young man. He was also advised to rethink his aspirations of working in the operating room until he was tested for MH.

At some point in this exam/interview, you will be invited to open your mouth as wide as you can; you will also be asked to tilt your head back as far as it will go. Your anesthesiologist is checking on how easy or difficult it will be to intubate you. Intubation is the placement of an endotracheal (breathing) tube into your airway so the anesthesiologist can help you breathe while you are under general anesthesia. I will address intubation further once we get you into the operating room. First let's talk about that great mood changer: the consent form.

Informed Consent

Nothing seems to wreck the mood and atmosphere more than the anesthesia consent form. I have seen it time and again. Your anesthesiologist is going over all the particulars I stated previously; the mood is not jovial, but it is light and casual. There may even be some laughter as you and your family interact with the medical staff around you. Then your anesthesiologist starts discussing your consent for anesthesia...

Before you receive anesthesia for your surgery, your anesthesiologist must obtain your written permission. This is fine until he starts to list all the things that may go wrong: *the risks of anesthesia.*

This always reminds me of those beautiful drug commercials on TV. They're talking about the benefits of this great drug... *the man is walking through the park with his grandson, holding his hand; soft, soothing music is playing... it's a beautiful spring day and you're on this life-changing drug.* Then a voiceover comes on above the soft music and lists countless medical tragedies that can result when you're on this medication!

Well, that's how it is with the anesthesia informed consent you must sign. Your anesthesia provider goes through a litany of mishaps and complications that can happen while you are under anesthesia: stroke, heart attack, paralysis — *and, yes, the list does end with the possibility of death.*

Signing this consent usually brings home the seriousness of surgery and all its associated risks. Your anesthesiologist is not trying to scare you right before your operation. This is just one necessary hurdle that must be dealt with because we live in such a litigious society. I have always wished that this consent could be signed in the surgeon's office when you sign your surgical consent; the risks and the conversations are very similar; however, your surgery is weeks away, so the mental impact is not as traumatizing.

As you listen to your anesthesiologist list all these adverse reactions and complications, remember that soothing drug commercial. It also contains many severe complications, yet, as you know logically, thousands of individuals take that drug and do just fine. Need further proof and reassurance? Look at the warnings on one of the most widely used drugs in America: *ibuprofen.* Its warnings list hives, shock, asthma, blisters, ulcers, and bleeding. Yet millions of people take this drug, some almost daily, with no complications.

Pre-Op Lines: IV's and A-Lines

As previously mentioned, your pre-op nurse will most likely place an IV and start you on IV fluids. This will be the first of about four to six lines you will receive. The second catheter you will most likely receive will be placed by either your anesthesia P.A. or your anesthesiologist. This line is *usually* placed in the pre-op area. This is a unique *arterial line* positioned in your radial or wrist artery. It is used to continuously measure your blood pressure. When you put your fingers on your wrist and feel your pulse, that is your radial artery. This small "IV-type" catheter can be inserted into that artery and when connected to a monitor, can accurately display your blood pressure second by second. This way, if your blood pressure changes for any reason at all, your surgical staff will notice. This line is a bit harder to place than your IV, so please be patient and try not to pull away. You will be given a local anesthetic to numb your wrist area. All other lines should, in most circumstances, be placed after you are asleep. *Yay!*

Please note: Some hospitals may place your A-line in the O.R. after you are sound asleep.

Circulating Nurse Interview

Just when you thought you could not handle one more interview, along comes your circulating nurse. *This should be your last round of questions before you are wheeled into the operating room.*

The circulating nurse is the nurse who will be with you for your entire operation. He or she will be the one responsible for all the surgical medications, instruments, machines, and products needed for your surgery. This nurse will be your liaison between the surgeon, your family, and all the other departments with which you will be associated — the blood bank, the ICU, the chemistry lab. He/she, along with a surgical technologist, will have set up the entire operating room prior to your arrival. All the surgical instruments, medications, valves, and sterile drapes, towels, and gloves will be under his/her care and domain. The circulating nurse and the surgical tech are both experts on what the surgeon requires.

It is their job to anticipate anything the surgical case or the surgeon may need. The circulating nurse's biggest responsibility, however, is to be your advocate. When you are anesthetized or sedated, you are powerless to make decisions on your own. The circulating nurse's role is to ensure your safety at a time when you are most vulnerable. If she sees or anticipates anything that may endanger your dignity, modesty, and most importantly, your physical safety, it is her job to speak out and prevent this from happening.

Here's an Insider's Secret:

Your family members are always within their rights to ask the circulating nurse for updates throughout the surgical case. Most circulators are happy to place one or two phone calls during the surgery. Moreover, with the advent of cell phones, these calls are easy and direct. It gives a family great solace and peace of mind to get an occasional update. To have to sit waiting hour after hour, not knowing what is happening to your loved one is, to me, distressful and unnecessary. And remember, your circulating nurse is always just a few feet away from the patient!

On a four- to six-hour case, I personally, as a circulating nurse, will usually call and inform the family of our progress at least three times. They are always appreciative and grateful for the update, and it takes only seconds out of my day.

She will once again probably ask those often-repeated questions: *"When was the last time you had anything to eat or drink?* and *"Have you had anything to drink or eat after midnight?"* I promise this should be the last time you are asked these questions!

If you can get out of any hospital with this question being asked of you fewer than 10,000 times, you will have set a record! But seriously, it is all about safety. Each practitioner you encounter is a participant in a plan of checks and balances set up to ensure your safety. No one wants to give you any substance or medication that can cause you to have an adverse reaction. So please be patient as we bother you with questions! Also, please notify us if anything has changed with your health status or medications since your initial pre-op history and physical.

Many patients do not have a clear understanding of the first important question: *"Have you had anything to drink or eat after midnight?"* When you hear hospital personnel talking, they will refer to this as NPO (nil per os), which means "nothing by mouth" to eat or drink. It is crucial that you have an empty stomach for at least eight hours before surgery and anesthesia. This ensures that either your nerves or the anesthesia medicine do not cause you to vomit. When you are sedated, you lose your natural gag reflex, thus increasing your risk of pulmonary aspiration. Aspiration (your stomach contents being vomited up and entering your lungs) is a very serious complication — one that can be avoided if you are NPO at least at eight hours before anesthesia.

Follow your doctor's instructions precisely. * Even a tiny sip of coffee or a nibble of food within that forbidden time period will cause the anesthesiologist to cancel your surgery. **There is no leeway on this one important point!**

> We once had a patient who really couldn't grasp the concept of not eating before surgery. He wanted to know when, what, and how he should eat before his operation. Finally, in exasperation, the surgeon told him, "Do not eat anything before you come to the hospital the day of your surgery." The patient followed the doctor's orders exactly and did not eat anything **before** coming to the hospital; however, once here he couldn't resist stopping in the hospital cafeteria and having a full breakfast of eggs and toast! Needless to say, all the O.R. staff in the room that day suddenly had an extra four hours in their schedule...

Most patients understand the question about allergies to medicines. However, I do see some confusion on patients' faces when they are asked whether they are allergic to Latex. I always ask my patients: *"Are you allergic to Latex? Rubber gloves, balloons — do they bother you in the form of rashes or breathing problems?"*

In the operating room, there are several items made from natural latex products: rubber. Latex is a natural rubber made from a rubber tree, *Hevea brasiliensis*. The two most common latex items are the surgical gloves used by the surgeons and the Foley catheter placed in the patient to keep his/her bladder empty of urine.

Although it is not widely known or talked about by the public, a small population of people are allergic to Latex. Their allergic reactions can range from a mild skin rash to life-threatening reactions, called *anaphylaxis*. If you are severely allergic to Latex and are exposed to it, your immune system overreacts to the "allergen," thus causing a severe reaction. These symptoms are life-threatening. Your throat can close, causing breathing problems, and your blood vessels can severely dilate, causing low blood pressure. For this population of patients, the surgical staff goes to great lengths to ensure that all gloves, Foley catheters, and other surgical items are *Latex free*.

Several of my patients will answer that they are not sure if they are allergic to Latex or rubber. *I assure them that if they were allergic, they would know it.* Wearing rubber gloves or blowing up a party balloon would have caused a reaction that would have been very noticeable to them at some point in their lives. Those who are at risk for Latex allergies are usually individuals who have been exposed to Latex repeatedly: healthcare workers and those who had several operations as a child, such as spina bifida patients.

Your circulating nurse will check your chart and peruse your history. He or she will also make sure your consent form is filled out correctly and signed by you, your surgeon, and your anesthesiologist. *Before the circulating nurse leaves, make sure your family asks him/her for one or two phone call updates; it makes their wait so much easier.* A few more of the same questions and you will be ready to head off to the O.R.

So, let's get going ... finally!

Steven Monteiro RN

A Kiss Good-Bye:

I once had a patient we were taking to the O.R. from the pre-op
area; he said goodbye to his family and his wife wished him good
luck. Just as we turned the corner and headed LEFT to our
operating suite, I heard her exclaim, "Oh, I forgot to kiss him
goodbye!" We paused to look back as she turned RIGHT, caught
up to a different stretcher, leaned over, and kissed some strange
man right on the lips! As she pulled away, realizing that this was
not her husband, she screamed, "OH NOOO!" The laughter from
all parties was, to say the least, uncontrollable. The 70-year-old
stranger commented that it was the most action he'd seen in years!

The Operating Suite

The first comment most patients usually make when
entering the operating room is about how cold it is. Truth
be told, most O.R.'s are on the cool side. However,
remember that all you have on for clothing is a thin paper
gown. If you ask your circulating nurse why it is so cold,
he/she may go into a discourse on how low temperatures
and low humidity reduce the bacteria level in the operating
room. This is a common fallacy (that may have *some*
merit). The truth of the matter is, *it is cold in the O.R. for
the comfort of the surgeon and staff.* While operating on
you, the surgeon and staff each wear a hat, a mask, a gown,
and rubber gloves. They also wear non-breathable shoe
covers that can make their feet very warm. This, along with
the hot operating room lights above them and the stress of
having your life in their hands, makes for a hot four to six
hours.

I always warm the room right before the patient arrives
and then turn the temperature down once my patient is
draped and covered. Studies have shown that a warm
patient will experience less bleeding and fewer infections,
so it is in everyone's interest to keep the patient as warm

36

as possible.

Now, if you are an astute patient, you may be saying to yourself, "Wait a minute, my doctor told me they were going to cool my body down while I was having heart surgery." *Oh, you caught me!* Yes, for certain open heart procedures your body is cooled down about 10 degrees. This cooling is meant to protect your heart tissue while you are on the cardio-pulmonary machine, which will be mentioned in more detail soon. However, once you are off the heart-lung machine, your body temperature is raised back to normal.

Your circulating nurse will give you a nice warm blanket and have you move onto the operating table. Most patients comment on how the table is so narrow. The table is purposely narrowed because a wider table would make it hard for the surgeon to reach you. He needs to be as close as possible to operate on you.

It is normal to be nervous when going into the operating room. It is a new environment, and *you are having surgery*. It would be abnormal not to have some jangled nerves. We will do everything we can to calm you down and make you comfortable. Unfortunately, we do descend on you like a pit crew at the *Indianapolis 500*. There will probably be three to five people approaching you all at once. Your nurse will be covering you with a blanket; he/she will also be placing a seat belt around your thighs. (We don't want you to roll off your table while falling asleep!) Your anesthesiologist and assistants will be hooking up your IV's, and someone will be placing cold EKG stickers all over you to monitor your heart. Someone may even start to shave some of the hair off your body. *Just when you think this is all way too much,* your anesthesiologist will say, "I'm going to give you something to help you relax..."

*Next thing you know, you are safe and sound, waking up
in the recovery room, ICU.*

Will I Wake Up in The Middle of Surgery?

*Every once in a while, there are stories in the news about patients
who have awakened in the middle of surgery.*

Does this really happen? In all my years of surgery I have never
had a patient fully wake up in the middle of surgery, and neither
have my colleagues. Do patients become "light" during surgery?
Yes; as the anesthetic gasses wane or as the surgeon works around
sensitive areas of the body, a patient will stir or start to move.
However, there is always a minimum of four people in direct
contact with that patient, and as soon as he or she starts to stir,
someone will state, "The patient is moving a bit." The
anesthesiologist will then provide more anesthetic and right back
to sleep the patient will go. On being fully awakened and
extubated, the patient is never aware that he stirred a bit during
his operation.

While You Were Sleeping

Before an operation, most patients do not want to know
what is going to happen to them surgically. However, once
they have returned home and felt all their scars and
wounds, they start to have some questions. So, let's briefly
touch on why you have the wounds you will have post-op.

The very first thing placed in you once you are asleep is the
endotracheal tube. When you are given the sedating drugs,
you no longer have the ability to breathe on your own. This
tube, when hooked to an oxygenator machine, will keep
your lungs breathing in air (oxygen). Unfortunately, the
endotracheal tube is also the tube that gives you a sore
throat once it is removed in the ICU.

When you are totally anesthetized, a bigger IV will be
placed in your neck. I know that this panics many people,

but it is a very safe area in which to place an IV. Your neck IV (jugular vein) is so large and so close to the heart that it allows greater volumes of fluid and medicine to be given to you. It is also through this catheter that your anesthesiologist will be able to place a Swan-Ganz catheter. This special catheter will give your doctors minute-by-minute information about everything from how well your heart is working to how much oxygen is in your blood. This IV, along with this particular catheter (Swan-Ganz), is an excellent adjunct that your doctors will use to keep you safe during your operation.

A Foley catheter will be placed through your urethra and into your bladder to drain your urine. The amount of urine produced during and after surgery is accurately measured and is a good indicator of how well your kidneys are working. It is also a good indicator of fluid balance — how hydrated you are at any given moment. This Foley catheter does not seem to bother women as much as it bothers men. Upon awakening, most men find it a great discomfort. These men cannot wait until it is removed! The Foley catheter for both males and females is usually removed at the end of day one or day two.

Also, especially for men, when they wake up, the catheter makes them feel as if they have to pee. No matter how much we tell them, "Just go! You have a catheter in you," until they are fully awake, they do not understand, and this is a great disconcert to them.

Your Incisions

If you touch yourself in the middle of your chest, you will feel a hard bone called your sternum. Behind your sternum is your heart. Your surgeon will cut straight through the middle of your sternum to access your heart. (For those who really need to know, yes, he does use a saw to cut through the bone, much like a hand-held reciprocating saw.) From there he will be able to place whatever catheters he needs to put you on the heart-lung machine. Once the machine is breathing and circulating your blood for you, the surgeon can then perform your scheduled operation.

Who Is Actually Doing the Cutting?

If your surgery happens to be performed in a teaching hospital (a place where residents or fellows learn medicine and surgery), the question may arise: *Is my surgeon actually doing the operation?*

In open heart surgery, in every single case I have been part of for 30 years, the answer has *always* been yes. Heart surgery is complicated and the surgeon is always in the control seat. If a resident or fellow is present, he may do some suturing and tying, and even some cutting, but the surgeon is right there doing the majority of the operation and is in **total control**.

The best response I ever heard to this question came from a surgeon I greatly respect. When asked if he had a resident or fellow with him and, if so, who would be doing the operation; his response was that, yes, he did have a fellow who would be assisting him. He then reminded this family that he was also once a fellow, and it was under the direction and tutelage of another surgeon that he became the surgeon this family had come to admire and trust with the life of their loved one.

Having said all that, you are within your rights to ask your surgeon to not have a resident operate on you. However, remember that a residency and most fellowships are a minimum of two years, and during those years your surgeon and his fellow have most likely developed a well-tuned routine that is beneficial to the patient and the surgical procedure. I have seen for decades how complementary this relationship can be. A great surgeon and a great fellow makes for a formidable surgical team!

However, not all heart surgeries require that the patient be placed on the heart-lung machine; some modern operations known as "off-pump" are performed without the use of cardiopulmonary bypass. In off-pump surgery, you are not placed on the heart-lung machine. In its simplest explanation, one of the main reasons for putting a patient on the heart-lung machine is to be able to stop the heart (to work on it) while still being able to circulate oxygenated blood to the patient's body and vital organs.

A perfusionist is present (this is the person who runs the heart-lung machine), but only in case he/she is needed to place you on the pump. In off-pump surgery, your surgeon does all your coronary bypasses while your heart is beating. If you are having valve replacement surgery, it will be necessary to place you on the heart-lung machine. Your valves are inside your heart, and the surgeon must open your heart to access them, whereas coronary bypasses are on the outside of the heart.

I have had patients ask, *"Why is there an incision in my leg if they were operating on my heart?"* For many patients, this leg incision is more troublesome and irritating after surgery than their chest incisions. If you are having coronary artery bypass surgery, your surgeon (or, more likely, your doctor's P.A.) will make an incision in your leg to harvest your saphenous vein. They can take more than 15 inches of the vein and use it on your heart to bypass your blocked heart vessels. *And, yes, you can live fine without this vein in your leg.* In fact, it is the same vein many women (and some men) have removed when they start to develop painful varicose veins in their legs.

Will I Need a Blood Transfusion?

The answer to that question is, most likely, yes. With the exception of *off-pump* surgery, most heart patients do receive blood and/or blood products during their operations. However, the blood used today in the United States is very safe and generally free from disease. It is extremely rare to get any type of disease through a blood transfusion. Today's blood is carefully tested and tracked extensively. The most common occurrence is an allergic reaction to a blood transfusion, and even that event is statistically low. More than five million people a year safely receive blood transfusions in the United States.

You may also find an incision in your arm; here your surgeon will have removed your radial artery (the same artery you felt in your wrist when we were talking about your A-line placement). Although used much less frequently, this artery can also be placed on your heart for bypasses.

There are two main arteries in the lower part of your arm: the radial and the ulnar. The ulnar, in most cases, is sufficient enough to supply adequate blood to your hand if the radial artery is removed. (Your surgeon or his P.A should have performed a simple test called an *Allen's Test* in his office to determine if your radial artery can be harvested). However, if you have medical problems such as carpal tunnel, Reynaud's, or overall poorly perfused hands (they go numb easily in cold weather), you will most likely have failed the *Allen's Test* and this artery is not a viable candidate for removal.

When your operation is completed, your surgeon will place two or three chest tubes in you to drain any blood and fluid that can accumulate in your chest cavity. These drains will also help keep your lungs expanded. The surgeon may also put temporary pacemaker wires on your heart to help it beat.

(Both the chest tubes and the pacemaker wires are removed once you're in the recovery room and stable. Their removal does not warrant another operation; they are just gently pulled out while you are on the medical floor.)

Your surgeon will then use thick-gauged wires to pull your sternum back together. He will use absorbable sutures to close your skin areas and will start to get your ready to go to the ICU.

Please forgive me, but I have purposely left this section vague in its details (except for mentioning the sternal saw). This book was written to ease your anxiety and give you an inkling of what to expect when having open heart surgery. To get into all the details of your surgery, which some may find gruesome, is not my intent. You chose your surgeon; you met him and by now you trust in his surgical skills. We should leave the surgical details to him and now concentrate on your recovery in the ICU.

See you there!

Do They Play Music in the O.R? Many people picture the operating room as a quiet sanctuary where the only sound is the rhythmic, tranquil beeping of the heart monitor. *Wrong!*

Music is a big part of the operating room. The iPhone or radio is always on, and the music can vary from country to rock to hip-hop. Some surgeons like the music blasting, while some like it at reasonable volumes.

I have had some surgeons (for some reason it always seems to be the orthopedic docs) who play hard rock so loud I can barely hear them ask for things. In my room, I like the music just loud enough that if you want to hear it you can, but if you're concentrating you won't even notice it's on. When we start to close, I crank it a little louder for some "closing music."

There are studies that show patients are more relaxed and need less anesthesia when music is played in the O.R. However, that study probably wasn't done in the *heavy rock* ortho department!

Chapter 3: Post-Op ICU

Post-op, or *postoperative*, is the period after surgery. When you arrive to the Intensive Care Unit (ICU) after your surgery, you will start out on multiple IV medications to maintain your blood pressure and heart rate. You will also be on pain medication and sedation (calming) medication so that you will be comfortable. Because of these drugs, you will not initially remember coming to the ICU. In the ICU, your nursing staff will closely and frequently monitor all your tubes, drains, and wires. If anything abnormal occurs throughout your stay, your nurse should let your surgeon (as well as your cardiologist) know with a telephone call. Some issues can be fixed without the doctor coming to see you, so please don't be scared if you do not see your surgeon until the next scheduled time for his rounds. Your surgeon, cardiologist, and P.A. are still monitoring you by communicating with your nurses and reviewing your lab work, vital signs, and fluid measurements.

When you are settled into your ICU room and stable, your family will be allowed to visit. If your family has any questions, they can ask the nursing staff, which includes nurses, nursing aides, and patient care technicians. There are many different healthcare workers in the hospital. If you or a family member are ever unsure about a staff member's position or role, please ask.

A Word for Your Family:

I have over the years seen the shock and dismay as families come to see their loved ones for the first time. You are intubated, you are on a respirator; you have so many lines coming from you that you look like some sort of cyborg. *"It doesn't even look like him!"* I've heard that cry a million times.

Please try to remember, he or she has just had major surgery and his/ her face will most likely be very swollen. This is normal. It is a process and every hour that passes, your loved one is heading back toward the person you know and expect them to be. Be patient and try not to panic. Your calm demeanor will help your loved one not be so frightened.

Katherine from the *Surgery Open Heart* Facebook forum wrote to a fellow member about seeing her husband for the first time in the ICU:

Bless you, my hubby and [I] were in the hospital in Oct to a surprise open heart surgery to replace his mitral valve with a mechanical valve and a shave [of] his heart muscle.

I couldn't handle it when I first saw him after surgery in the ICU. I got sick to my stomach and dizzy and had to leave for a while to process it all and gather myself before going back in. He was out when I went in there that time, so I was thankful for that [as] I didn't want him to see me so upset. I had to be the rock and take care of him. So glad you're [through] the hard part take, it slow, don't rush the healing part.

The IV pumps, heart monitors, and many other pieces of medical equipment can make the ICU a very stimulating place, with lots of alarms and lights going off. Try your best to relax. Your arms may be tied to the bed's side rails with cloth ties (soft restraints) so that you do not accidentally pull out any of your necessary tubes. *Be aware of this before your surgery.* Some patients have stated that it was very scary to wake up with a tube in their throat and with their hands tied down. If this is a situation that may freak you out, be sure to talk to your doctor and find out exactly how you will be waking up. Most patients hardly remember, but others are very aware of being intubated and waking up on a breathing machine.

Once you can breathe on your own, your breathing tube will come out. It can often be removed within six to 12 hours, but it may have to stay in longer if complications arose during the surgery or if you have lung diseases. Once the breathing tube is out (extubated), you will be able to talk again; however, your throat will hurt because the breathing tube will have irritated your throat lining. You may still need oxygen after the breathing tube is removed. Your nurse will accomplish this via either a mask that covers your nose and mouth or small, soft prongs that go into your nose.

Most people, on average, stay in the ICU for a day or two. Much of this time is spent working hard to prevent post-op complications. You will be asked to do several things that you may not feel up to doing. You will be tired and achy, but your nursing staff will ask you to walk, wash up, and do breathing exercises. They will give you pain medication and try to make you as comfortable as possible while you do this hard work, but you may still feel achy. Trust me; they are not trying to Nurse Ratched punish you; this is asked of you because research has shown that all this hard work prevents complications and helps you recover smoothly after your big surgery.

Once you are extubated and breathing on your own, you will be given several deep breathing exercises. There is a natural tendency not to breathe in deeply when you feel the pain of your operation with each inspiration. Shallow breathing can cause the small airways in your lungs to close. To compound the situation (a catch-22 of sorts), the narcotic pain medication we give you also curtails your breathing. This condition sets you up for a lose-lose

47

situation, with the unfortunate result being the possibility of pneumonia.

To combat this complication, you will be given an *incentive spirometer*. This ingenious device exercises your lungs as you use it to take deep breaths. This spirometer will help open your small airways. Your nurse will teach you how to sit up and inhale from the spirometer, slowly and deeply, for as long as you can. You then hold that deep breath for a few seconds and exhale. (If you grew up in the 70's, this may be easy and reminiscent!) The spirometer is used 10 to 15 times every hour, so try not to fall behind!

When the spirometer opens your airways, you may have the urge to cough up phlegm. This is good! This opens your airways and prevents pneumonia. At the same time, coughing can cause pain and put pressure on your chest incision. This pain can be eased by "splinting" your cough — a technique you will be taught that involves hugging a pillow against your chest. Immediately post-op you may be afraid to cough, laugh, or sneeze. You will quickly learn to instinctively reach for your pillow to *splint* your chest. This unique pillow (sometimes it's red and in the shape of a heart) will become your close friend.

> **A Floor Nurse's Story:**
>
> While rounding on my patients one day, I stopped to listen to a patient's lung sounds with my stethoscope. His lungs didn't sound quite as good as I thought they should have been at that point in his recovery. I asked him if he had been using his incentive spirometer. He insisted he had been, so I asked him to show me how high he was getting it.
>
> He put it up to his mouth and exhaled hard and forcefully, with his cheeks puffing out so wide that Louie Armstrong would have been impressed. "It's broken!" he insisted. Holding in a laugh, I reminded him that you INHALE from it, not EXHALE. Now the spirometer worked! He knew that he had been caught ignoring his breathing exercises.

While in the hospital it is easy to fall off your daily hygiene routines, so you may be asked to brush your teeth twice daily. Oral hygiene is another measure taken to prevent pneumonia and other lung complications after surgery. You may even be given a special mouthwash to use throughout the day.

You will be instructed to not lie flat after surgery, as this can cause stomach juices to slide up and into your lungs, creating an aspiration risk. To prevent this, you will be encouraged to sit up in a chair whenever possible. Also, keeping the head of your bed elevated will help keep your lungs clear. However, the very best thing you can do is ambulate — get out of bed and walk around the ICU with your nurse or aide. Walking will help your lungs expand and your blood flow, preventing blood clots. Walking is so beneficial for healing after surgery that we try to get you up and walking as soon as possible. *Those old days of being sedentary in bed are gone for good!*

Any surgery — but especially open heart surgery, which places your blood through the heart-lung machine — increases your risk of blood clots. Walking, sequential compression devices and medications are all tools to prevent blood clots from forming.

Sequential compression devices are pneumatic sleeves that wrap around your legs, squeeze, and then relax. This mimics walking by pumping the blood back up to your heart so that your blood does not remain stagnant in your legs. Your nurse will place these sleeves on you whenever you are sedentary. Some patients find the constant massaging relaxing, while others find it annoying. *Which type of patient do you think you will be?*

A common medication used to prevent clots from forming is heparin. Heparin comes as an injection, usually given three times a day. Sorry — it does sting a bit! However, it trumps getting a blood clot somewhere in your body. The sting is less than a flu shot and, believe it or not, many patients eventually adjust to the routine of injections. Heparin does not come in a pill form. If you are on a routine of baby aspirin (low-dose 81-mg tablets), it is the same concept: the thinning of your blood.

You will be NPO again for a bit after surgery. *Sorry*. This is just in case something happens and you need to go back to the O.R. quickly. Once we are confident that you are recovering smoothly, you can start eating again. We will start you off with light foods. Anesthesia medications can cause post-op nausea (the feeling you are going to throw up) or actual throwing up. Light foods will help you adjust until the side effects of anesthesia wear off. Your blood sugar will be checked after each meal, and you may receive insulin medication to lower your blood sugar. This does not mean you went into surgery as a *non-diabetic* and came out with *diabetes*. It is just that medical science has realized over the years that maintaining a good blood sugar level after surgery is an important way of preventing infections and other complications. Having heart surgery causes your body to release stress hormones. These hormones interfere with your body's ability to utilize insulin effectively — you need insulin in order to regulate your blood sugar. Studies have shown that strict control of your blood sugar after heart surgery leads to lower infection rates and greater healing properties.

As you continue recovering in the ICU, your vital signs will frequently be taken. As you become more stable, the IV medications can be lessened, and the arterial lines and central IV lines can be removed. You will require at least a small IV catheter the entire time you are in the hospital so that you can receive fast-acting medications in the event of an emergency. You will be observed for abnormal heart rhythms that may occur after heart surgery. A few days after your surgery, the temporary pacing wires are removed with just a gentle tug.

Your blood will occasionally be drawn to check blood levels and make sure you are not experiencing post-op bleeding. Your electrolyte levels will be monitored, and you will be given electrolytes for any low concentrations. Your urine will frequently be measured to make sure your kidneys did not experience any complications during the surgery. The Foley catheter will be taken out when your urinary output is consistent. You will still need to urinate into a container for measurements.

At this point, you may find yourself constipated. Constipation is a known side effect of narcotic pain medication. Constipation can usually be relieved through walking, drinking fluids, increasing fiber intake, or using stool softeners. Don't be discouraged about this. Your nurse will help you, and having a bowel movement is one of the criteria for being released from most hospitals.

When the chest tube drainage decreases, the chest tubes are taken out. You are given instructions to take a deep breath, then hold it and bear down while the tubes are removed. *You are now almost home free!*

However *(why is there always a however?)*, I have to take a time out to discuss chest tube removals. This is by far one of the most controversial steps in the entire recovery process. Some doctors and institutions do not provide pain medication when removing chest tubes. They feel that since it takes only one second to pull each chest tube, pain meds are not needed. Some patients tolerate this non-medicated removal very easily. However, those who do not state that it was the worst pain they have felt in their lives. For these patients, the pain was so severe that even months later it was unforgettable. I read several articles on this subject and talked to many patients about their experiences. The conclusions are mixed and controversial. For some patients, it was a non-issue; for others, it was extremely painful.

Hine from *Surgery Open Heart Facebook* page writes:

"So my ICU nurse warned me that removing the drains was extremely painful. I took in as much painkillers as I could and she was so amazing it didn't hurt as much because she talked me through it."

You have been through enough, so you may want to ask about pains meds before having your chest tubes removed. In most cases, your nurse or doctor will suggest and offer pain meds, but if they don't, ask about them yourself and see what your doctor and nurse say about the situation. Most institutions will likely offer morphine or an equivalent IV pain reliever.

Your surgeons will continue to monitor your progress, and

while in the ICU you will also meet several other health-care advocates:

- **Respiratory Therapists** who will ensure that you are breathing well and using your spirometer or other breathing exercise tools.

- **Physical Therapists** and **Occupational Therapists** who will help you regain your mobility and skills after heart surgery in a way that is safe for your surgical incisions.

- **Dietitians** who will make sure you are meeting your nutrient requirements while healing from surgery.

- **Pharmacists** and **Pharmacy Technicians** who will prepare your medications and ensure that they are given in a safe manner

At this point, you should start making progress and slowly start feeling like yourself again. When your vital signs are stable and you require less-frequent assessments and monitoring, you will be transported to the inpatient ward. You will have to say goodbye to all the nurses and staff you have come to rely on and trust, but believe me — your new staff will be just as helpful and reliable.

Chapter 4: Inpatient Ward / Closer to Home

After being in the ICU for one or two days, you will be moved to a regular room on the inpatient ward for another two to five days. Here you will have fewer cords and drains to tie you down, and you will be expected to gradually increase your activity level. Moving around should be a bit easier for you, and you should start to require less pain medication to be comfortable. Here you will do more with your physical therapist and occupational therapist.

Your physical therapists (PTs) and occupational therapists (OTs) will teach you how to start performing your daily activities in a way that will protect your sternum. Remember, your sternum was the large breastbone that your surgeon had to saw through to reach your heart. *Yikes!* Yes, yikes indeed. This large bone is now wired together and, just like any broken (or sawed) bone, it needs time to heal and fuse back together. In fact, it requires weeks. No different from placing a broken leg in a cast for several weeks.

Your physical and occupational therapists will teach you how to avoid stressing that sternal bone until it fuses back together. They will teach you not to push on the arms of your chair to stand. Pushing with your arms can move the wires that are keeping your sternum together. They will teach you to cross your arms over your chest while standing; this will help you avoid the temptation to use your arms as you stand. They will also teach you to push your feet into the floor and use your leg muscles to stand.

You will also be instructed to not pull the grab bars in the bathroom to stand up from the toilet or move around in the shower. Using a raised toilet seat and a shower chair can help you get everything done without using your arms to pull. You will also practice going up and down stairs without pulling on the railing. *You'd be surprised how much you rely on pulling rails when climbing stairs.* All these strategies are used to keep your chest together until the bone heals.

During this time, try to avoid reaching behind your back. You will be surprised how much this affects your movement! You should not reach behind your back to tuck in your shirt or use your back pockets. You will need to position the toilet paper in an easy-to-reach place in the bathroom, and you may need help cleaning yourself in the bathroom. This can be embarrassing and frustrating. However, remember that every other patient on your floor is going through the same thing, and your nurse has been helping patients wipe themselves for most likely years. It is a necessary stage in your recovery, and if it helps you get home, we are glad to do it. Please know that it is our pleasure to assist you in the hospital, so don't be afraid to ask for help.

A gait belt may be placed around your waist while you are walking during PT and OT. This belt is wide and has handles or straps so that your therapist can get a better hold on you. This provides support if you are off balance and allows the therapist to help you stay upright a bit more easily. Your therapist will watch your posture as you walk through the hospital halls and give you tips if anything can be improved: "Look up, make your stance a bit wider"... this is all to prevent you from falling. You already have a fair amount of healing to do after your surgery. We do not want to add a fall!

You should start to sleep a bit better now that the bright lights and loud alarms of the ICU are gone. If you do start to have trouble sleeping, let the nursing staff know. They may be able to give you medications to help you relax or use other techniques like blocking out light or using earplugs. Sometimes sleep must be interrupted so that staff can measure vital signs or give medications; you can always work with the hospital staff to balance this with your sleep cycle. *You need sleep at night so that you have the energy to do all that is asked of you during the day.*

You should gradually start feeling a bit more like yourself. You will be able to eat a bit more, but your appetite may not be back to normal. Your dietitian will ask about the foods you like and dislike, as well as your food sensitivities/allergies and special diets you follow (e.g., vegetarian or kosher). He/she will combine these with your heart-healthy diet requirements to find a meal plan that meets all your needs. This diet will be low in sodium (salt). Sodium makes your body hold onto fluid. When your heart has more fluid to pump, it is under more stress. You will most likely be offered a low-sodium diet that you can follow while you enjoy your life at home.

Your nurses and dieticians will encourage you to eat as much of your meal as you can. You need protein to fight off infection and heal your wounds! Also, zinc and vitamin C are essential for new tissue growth, so you may be prescribed a multivitamin to take while your wounds heal.

Your nurses or doctors will change or remove the bandage over your chest and other incisions. You can help prevent infections of your wounds by washing your hands before touching your incision sites.

You may still be at risk for developing pneumonia and should continue using your incentive spirometer. The hospital staff will by now expect you to use your incentive spirometer on your own, without being prompted. Some patients use TV commercials as a cue to use their spirometers. Another breathing exercise tool you may be provided with is the *flutter valve*. This is a type of PEP (positive expiratory pressure) therapy. You wrap your mouth around the mouthpiece and exhale forcefully against the resistance of the machine. This exhalation creates pressure and vibrates your airways, dislodging mucus that would otherwise stay stuck in your airways, causing pneumonia to develop.

Your vital signs will become more stable and the frequent monitoring you were used to in the ICU should wane. Your nurses and doctors will still closely monitor your progress, however. Vital signs, lab results, chest X-rays, and your fluid intake and urinary output will still be taken, just less frequently. Hospital staff will listen to your heart and lungs and look at your incisions. Be sure to report any symptoms you are experiencing. Even if something seems minor and unrelated to your surgery, it could be an important clue for diagnosing a complication and treating it early.

Before you are discharged from the hospital, make certain that you understand any recommended medication changes. Your medications may have changed since your surgery. Your doctor may have you stop some of your medications and place you on new medicines. **Be sure to have a detailed discussion with your doctor about how you are going to handle the pain for the next few weeks and months.** This is a crucial subject and one that for most is not thoroughly discussed. Some doctors are very liberal with their pain medication prescriptions, while others are considerably more conservative.

Prescription pain medication addiction is a very real concern today.

No medical professional wants to be responsible for getting someone hooked on pain meds; on the other hand, it is hard to make a proper recovery when one is in constant pain. It is a great balancing act and the show is different for each individual.

Unfortunately, it is the opiate painkillers that offer the best pain relief. Oxycodone (Percocet), morphine, Vicodin, and codeine are commonly prescribed for pain. These drugs, though great for pain relief, are also very addictive. Many patients tend to believe that because their doctor prescribed these medicines, they must be safe. However, this nation is riddled with people who have become addicted to opiates that were at first a prescribed pain medication. So be sure to talk to your doctor while the two of you are together; it is much easier to have a frank discussion about pain abatement face to face with your doctor than to call weeks later stating that you are "still in constant pain" or worse yet, that you feel you are becoming "too dependent on your pain meds."

Also note: many pain meds (especially opioids) such as Vicodin can cause constipation; discuss with your doctor whether you should take an over-the-counter stool softener along with your medication. If he/she does prescribe something, be sure to take it as instructed. Constipation can sneak up on you, especially when you are on pain meds and somewhat dehydrated, so you want to definitely stay ahead of it. The consequences of not staying on top of this are what we nurses call "rectal intervention." Trust me; the first option is more desirable for all parties involved.

Remember to take your incentive spirometer with you; you may need it at home. You are still at risk for lung infections, and the pain you experience may keep you from breathing in deeply. *Oh and don't forget that splinter pillow, you don't want to leave your best friend behind!*

The very last thing that will happen is that your IV will be removed. You will then be allowed to change from your gown into your regular clothes.

Welcome back to the human race!

You will have an appointment with your surgeon and cardiologist to follow up and make sure you are healing well after surgery. You are out of the hospital but still recovering. Try to stay positive and focused. We are rooting for you to heal, and it's okay to take a few extra weeks to get back to being yourself!

Chapter 5: Home Sweet Home

As you ease back into your normal routines, it is even more important to practice your sternal precautions. As you get stronger, the urge to do tasks yourself will be tempting and subconscious. Your sternum is still not healed, so please be careful.

Wash your hands before touching your wound or dressing. Your doctor will most likely tell you to take showers rather than soak in a bathtub. Soaking exposes your incisions to more bacteria, so hot tubs and swimming pools should also be avoided. Most doctors will instruct you to let the soap and water run over your incision while showering; however, every wound heals differently, so follow your doc's instructions for when and how to shower.

Consider using a shower stool if you feel weak or unsteady. In the early stages, you will be surprised at how the simple act of showering can sap all your energy.

Pat dry your chest when you get out of the shower. Scrubbing or drying the incision vigorously can open the wound. Also, unless otherwise instructed, avoid using lotions or creams on your incisions until they heal. You may still have little band-aid type strips on your leg and chest called *steri-strips*. These will eventually fall off on their own, usually while you are showering. Follow your doctor's instructions on their removal if he/she tells you otherwise.

Depending on the surgical approach your surgeon used, your chest incision may have extended through the skin, muscle, and even bone. Your skin and muscle should heal much faster than your bone, with your breastbone taking at least eight weeks to recover. Tingling, numbness and itching are normal sensations and should wane over time. Women may find that wearing a comfortable bra helps minimize their chest discomfort. Some women purchase front-fastening bras before their surgery. You will most likely be instructed not to reach behind yourself while your sternum heals; a front-clasping bra solves this problem.

As you recover, expect to feel discomfort where you had incisions, especially as your activity increases. However, you should not experience the same pain you had before surgery — especially if you were having episodes of angina. If you do experience any of these pains, call your doctor immediately. Some sternal pops or cracks can be normal the first few days after surgery; however, if you feel as if your sternum is moving, let your doctor know.

If a vein was taken from your leg for bypasses, it might become swollen. Your doctor should have given you white TED support stockings; if he/she did, wear them according to his/her instructions. These stockings will significantly reduce your leg swelling and make your legs much more comfortable. Your doctor or his/her nurse should have also instructed you to remove them in the evening before going to bed; if these are your instructions, be sure to adhere to them.

You should have also received instructions to prop your feet higher than your heart when sitting. This elevation helps with leg swelling. Your best friend as you recover is walking. Walking will help with your leg circulation and your recovery. When your doctor feels that you are steady enough to start walking, try your best to follow his/her instructions. If you check the forum websites you will encounter further on in this book — patients praise the benefits of walking, and many use the distances as milestone markers for how well they are recovering.

Walking is such a great exercise because it increases circulation throughout your body. It is important, however, to increase your activity gradually. **Do not overdo it and do not walk alone!** Especially in the early weeks, make sure someone is there to help you physically and mentally as you start your walking journeys. Stop and rest as you feel the need. If you have extreme temperatures (heat waves or cold snaps), walk in an indoor environment. Cold weather limits your blood circulation and heat waves can sap your strength and vitality. Everyone progresses at different rates. Try to plan your day according to your energy reserves; if you walk and feel tired, take the time to rest and keep your energy secure. If you do too much, it will not benefit your recovery, and becoming weak can cause you to fall. A fall is the last setback you need in this recovery!

The best advice I have heard from other heart patients is to *listen to your body*. It will tell you how much to do and when you need rest. Don't try to set unrealistic milestones. Setbacks are inevitable, especially if you push yourself more than you should. In time, you will be ready for cardiac rehab, and that will help you immensely, not only physically but emotionally and psychologically too. These same patients also advise: "*get dressed every day.*" Staying in your bathrobe every day just because you're homebound can have a profound effect on your psyche. Getting dressed daily is telling yourself that you are getting back to normal and ready to do your usual activities.

It will still be necessary to splint your chest with a pillow when you cough or sneeze; by now you should be an expert at this. Move carefully and if you feel any pulling on the sternum, stop the activity you are doing. Avoid raising your arms over your head. (If you get held up at gunpoint, explain your surgery; most robbers will understand.)

Your doctor or discharge nurse will instruct you not to lift anything weighing more than five to 10 pounds. (A gallon of milk weighs around eight to nine pounds.) Use the special techniques learned from your physical and occupational therapy sessions. Ask for help when you are unable to reach or lift something. These limitations can be in place for two months while your sternum heals but always go by your doctor's guidelines and constraints.

Gesundheit: Watch Out for That First Sneeze!

A patient once told me that the first time he sneezed after open heart surgery sent him straight to the floor. "It was like someone had shoved a knife right into my chest. It was blinding agony!"

Even two-month post-surgery patients say it can be extremely painful and frightening. So be aware and prepared.

Try to have your splint pillow close by. Over time you will learn to ease your sneezes and not have those big explosive sneezes we enjoy. Eventually, most patients learn the best way to let out their sneezes. And stay encouraged; every day that passes heals your sternum just a little bit more until that one day when you can sneeze again — loud, explosive, and yes, even enjoyable.

Now that you have a new and repaired heart, this is an excellent time to start a healthy diet, one rich in fiber, fruits, and vegetables and low in fat, salt, and sugar. If you smoked before your surgery, now would be a good time to stop. Discuss it with your doctor— nicotine patches are just one alternative.

Before you know it, you will gradually be able to return to your normal routines. Check with your doctor for the right time to resume these activities. Be diligent, watch for signs of wound infection, and report any changes to your doctor. Signs include:

- Swelling, redness, and warmth around the wound

- Excessive pain when the wound is touched

- Leaking from the incision that smells bad or looks yellowish, greenish, or bloody

- Opening at the wound site

- Fever

- Trouble breathing

- Nausea or vomiting

- Persistent cough

- Dizziness

- Difficulty in breathing

- Extreme fatigue

If you are skinny or petite you may be able to feel your sternal wires under the skin; it will be a raised bump every few inches going down your chest. This is normal. The concern comes into place if you start to see them protruding through your skin; if so notify your doctor immediately.

Even though your surgery is done and the initial problem is fixed, you can still be at risk for heart-related health concerns in the future. Pay attention to how your body feels. Be sure to report any new chest pain or trouble breathing. Palpitations, rapid heart rate, nausea, vomiting, indigestion, or pain traveling to your jaw, neck, or back aɪ all reasons to contact your doctor immediately.

You may be instructed to weigh yourself at the same time daily while wearing the same amount of clothing. A weight gain of two pounds or more in 24 hours can be a sign of fluid overload and must be reported to your doctor.

You may become keenly aware of your heart beating, your chest breathing, and muscle tension throughout your body. This is normal. Your mind is focused on your recovery and symptoms, so this is good. Eventually, this realization will fade, and you will go back to noticing your external environment more than your internal environment.

Who you going to call?

Should I call my surgeon or my cardiologist if I have a problem after I return home?

The general consensus is that if it's surgically related (wound problems, sternal clicking, possible infection) you should call your surgeon.

However, you will most likely be placed back under the care of your cardiologist and all questions about your heart (rhythms, pain, medications) will probably be best addressed by him.

In fact, most patients are instructed to see their cardiologist 2 weeks after surgery and see their cardiac surgeon 4 weeks post-op.

Pericarditis

One common complication after open heart surgery is pericarditis. This is where the lining of the heart becomes inflamed. One of the symptoms of this inflammation is sharp chest pain which may become worse when you lie

ıthe in and that gets better when you sit
e symptoms, along with a fever, are the
‿‿ ʋr pericarditis. Call your doctor immediately
ıı you are experiencing these symptoms. It usually does not
mean re-hospitalization and can often be managed with
medication.

One heart patient described her pericarditis pain as
"horrendous." She stated that her pain was *"deep* and
radiated just like an MI." She went on to say that she could
not *"take a deep breath or lie flat."*

The American Heart Association wisely warns that the
"common symptom of pericarditis is chest pain." They
state that this can feel like a heart attack. They further
warn that one should seek emergency help right away
because the distinction between the two is so slight that
one may indeed be having a heart attack.

Depression and Mood Changes

Significant life changes occur as a result of heart surgery;
depression is common. Let me say that again: *depression
is common after surgery.* It's not that you are weak. It's
not that you are different. It is a mental and chemical
response to all the stress your body has endured.

Some studies show that as many as 40 percent of patients
experience clinical depression after heart surgery. That is
a significantly high percentage! Depression, however, is
not to be confused with sadness. You may experience
sadness after surgery. You may even feel defeated,
especially if your recovery is slower or harder than you
expected. What separates depression from sadness is that
depression tends to linger for weeks. It tends to manifest
as a loss of interest or pleasure in things you would
normally enjoy. Granted, post-heart surgical patients are

66

not able to enjoy the activities they previously enjoyed, but as time goes by and you feel yourself getting back to "normal," your mood should coincide with these milestones. If it does not, you may be experiencing a bout of depression and should consult your doctor. Remember, although depression is a *mental ailment*, it does have a direct *physical impact* on your recovery. Patients with depression may experience higher blood pressure, increased platelet counts, and increased hormone levels. If left untreated, depressed cardiac patients are at an increased risk for a cardiac event compared to post-op patients that are not depressed.

The good news, however, is that depression is treatable. Psychological and medical interventions are available, so don't try to *"tough it out alone."* Seek ways to reduce your stress and improve your mood. Embrace the help and support of friends and family during your recovery. Let your doctor know if you continue to experience depression, irritability, or sadness. Remember, this is normal and not something to be ashamed of — you are stronger than you may realize. Also, pay close attention to the *Cardiac Rehab* program coming up in the next section. There you will find physical and emotional support as well as camaraderie from patients who are experiencing exactly what you are going through. Trust me; you are not alone!

On one of the heart forums in which I participate, someone asked about a mood change in her husband after heart surgery. She was concerned because he could not remember events leading from the emergency room to the cath lab to even his bypass surgery. However, she was most concerned about his poor attitude and negativity. She asked: *Will this continue? What as a spouse can I do to help him?*

Gail, a longtime member of this heart forum and a quadruple bypass and mitral valve replacement patient herself, offered some great advice. She gracefully gave me permission to share it in this book:

I think this is all very normal. During his time in hospital, he was very heavily drugged and also during the surgery, he was on anesthetics. I remember very clearly some events in the hospitals and others are a blur. Some of my recollections are totally different than what my family remembers. My mind was not working right, and I knew it, but the doctors and nurses in the hospital told me that was normal after surgery and reassured me that it was only temporary. They were right, but it takes time.

When I got out of [the] hospital, I felt nauseous, was in a lot of pain and suffering from anxiety. I just felt like throwing up the whole time and people were telling me to eat and to take all these pills. Well, it is very difficult to feel positive when you feel so lousy 24/7. The only thing you can look forward to is more of the same the next day. Once I got off the heavy pain meds and switched to just Extra Strength Tylenol, I started to feel a bit better.

My husband and children were very supportive, although I did not show appreciation at the time. But what really helped me make it through is that they kept reminding me that it will get better, and I am not going to feel this bad forever.

Right now the most important thing for his body [is] to mend itself. He will have lots of time in the future to work on proper diet and exercise. The things that are important now [are] that he eat, walk, use the spirometer and get lots of rest.

You can help by being there for him. Let him eat whatever he wants and don't nag him. Keep reminding him that things will get better. Sympathize with him when he doesn't want to walk or use the spirometer but insist that he has to. Remind him that the more he walks, the faster he will recover and the easier it will get. Point out small accomplishments as each one is proof he is gradually getting better.

You will probably feel that [as] he starts to feel better his spirits will lift, and his attitude will improve. Let him recover at his own pace. One thing that bugged me is that people would either say outright or imply that if they had the same surgery, they would recover faster and work harder on getting better. That is easy to say when you are not the one going through it. It made me feel like it [was] all my fault that I felt so bad.

Gail

A Note to Caregivers and Family:

Family members need to know that personality changes may occur after someone has had heart surgery. Some patients become depressed while others become angry or emotional.

I have known patients who have never outwardly cried in front of their families but who suddenly became weeping messes. Some patients who have never been hostile or bitter are suddenly mad all the time.

Because you are a loved one, unfortunately, all these emotions may be displaced toward you. That old saying "We tend to hurt the ones we love" is very appropriate here. Try to be patient and understanding without turning a blind eye to your loved one's emotional stability. If you feel that things are getting out of hand or too hard to handle, seek help. Don't be embarrassed about turning to other family members or talking to your doctor. Most medical professionals are aware of these issues and early intervention will not only help you but will also benefit your loved one.

Surgeon **Marc Wallack** has a great eight-step plan for recuperating from heart surgery. Take a look at his article in *US News Health* on the web: *Recuperating From Heart Surgery: An 8-Step Comeback Plan.* Google his name and "8 Step Comeback" and it should pop up. He experienced chest pain while training for a marathon and needed immediate emergency surgery. Even with all his medical knowledge, he still had fears, both founded and unfounded. If you have fears and depression, this article will be very enlightening.

Wallack's article also talks about the fear of having sex after a heart attack. He admits that he was *worried about dying during sex* and also about whether he had the *physical strength to perform.* All well-founded fears one might have after heart surgery, but a subject many are reluctant to discuss with their doctors. Dr. Wallack's article advises heart patients: *"don't ignore the sex issue."* Ask your doctor when it is safe to resume your sex life and be honest about any fears you may have relating to sex. Wallack also has a book on Amazon called *Back to Life After a Heart Crisis.* I have not read it, but it has excellent reviews.

You must continue following up with your doctor to monitor the status of your heart, but by now you should be solidly on the road to recuperation. Your cardiologist will most likely offer and prescribe *cardiac rehabilitation.* If this is provided, try to take full advantage of it. If it is not offered or discussed, bring it up with your doctor.

Cardiac Rehab

Cardiac rehabilitation is a medically supervised program designed to help get you back to an active and safe physical lifestyle. Many insurance plans, including Medicare, provide coverage for cardiac rehabilitation. Its primary goal is to offer counseling, exercise, nutrition, and psychological support as you recover.

As they are instructed to start their road to rehabilitation, many patients are reluctant and even scared to stress their bodies. They feel that any physical strain or stress may injure them or cause another heart attack or problem. This is why cardiac rehab is such a great program. While you participate in the program, you are under the care and supervision of skilled staff: cardiac nurses, a physical therapist, exercise physiologists, and a nutritionist. All of them have specific knowledge of your surgery and limitations and all are trained in cardiac and emergency patient care. Best of all, your progress is reported back to your doctor.

At cardiac rehab, you are given more tools and information to keep your heart healthy. Don't think of it as a bunch of senior citizens trudging on a half-broken treadmill. Most of these places are vibrant and modern. The course can include swimming, bicycling, and walking programs. *(It's not your father's cardiac rehab!)* You learn how hard and how much you can stress and exercise your body. They teach you how to alternate periods of rest and activity so that you can exercise without getting too fatigued. You will also have the opportunity to meet others who are on the same journey and who maybe even had the same surgery. You will learn how to get the best results out of all your hard work.

As you exercise, the cardiac rehab staff will monitor not only your heart rate but also your EKG pattern. Most centers have monitors that measure your vital signs, oxygen saturation, and blood pressure. *Now that's a safe way to start exercising and stressing your heart!*

Other benefits of cardiac rehabilitation include:

- Detection and control of irregular heartbeats
- Detection and monitoring of post-op complications
- Review of your medications and dietary supplements
- Direct communication with your physician
- Education on how to lower your LDL bad cholesterol and raise your HDL good cholesterol
- Maintenance of your weight or weight loss
- Education on the risk factors of your surgery and recovery
- Education on healthy lifestyle changes: smoking cessation, daily exercise, diet
- Slowing or even reversing cardiovascular disease

- Improvement of your physical fitness, energy level, and heart strength

Unfortunately, many patients do not participate in cardiac rehab. Among those who do, many drop out long before the end of the program. Some of the main reasons for non-participation are lack of transportation, lack of strong endorsement from one's doctor, high insurance co-pay, and issues with accessibility to the cardiac rehab site. The programs are usually two or three one-hour sessions per week, and the program can be as long as 36 weeks. It is the length of the program that I believe is the main stumbling block for most patients. I have heard patients state that after the first couple weeks they had learned what to do and were capable of doing it on their own at home. However, just like most gym memberships (trust me, I used to be a personal fitness trainer), most people drop out of exercise programs after one month, especially if they are trying to do it on their own.

Here is a conversation about cardiac rehab between two *Facebook* members (Cara and Michael) on our group discussion page, *Surgery Open Heart*:

Michael: *Cardiac rehab is a MUST.... this is the greatest opportunity to get yourself back on your feet SAFELY and with all the monitors that keep track of your progress — you will never be able to replace that at this level, so do it as long as you can. Fortunately, my gym was not only a part of the hospital system but was a regular gym that anyone can join, so you can stay on if you want. After eight weeks of rehab, they put me back on weights. Talk about getting back to normal; this was great... Do whatever you can to take advantage of it. Plenty of time to get back to workouts on your own.*

Cara: *Did they monitor your heart rate and rhythm*

while on a bike or walking/jogging?

Michael: *Yes, I just hooked myself up after I checked in and it was routine. Heart rate was always being monitored, and I would sit after my workout until they monitored my resting heart rate. Was a top-notch facility.*

In another *Facebook* heart forum, Matt answers a patient's question about whether or not to do cardiac rehab :

It was an absolutely essential part of my recovery, both physical and mental. By the 6th week, after a rehab session I felt like I could climb a mountain. Need to get back on track again, sadly. I was back to work as a firefighter four months after CABG X 4, at age 39.

The statistics from the American Heart Association are sobering. Only 31 percent of post-cardiac-bypass patients participate in cardiac rehab programs. However, those who do attend and complete the entire program have a 20 to 30 percent reduction in mortality up to five years post participation. One study of more than 21,000 patients revealed a 17 percent reduction in recurrent heart attacks in patients who took advantage of cardiac rehab programs; it also showed a 47 percent reduction in death at two years out over those who did not do cardiac rehab. *That statistic alone should give you pause.*

Bottom line: if you are offered cardiac rehab, and your insurance covers it, *take advantage of it*! Studies clearly show that those who attend all sessions (usually around 36) are less likely to die or have a heart attack in the next four years than those who do not attend. The camaraderie alone will be worth it. You will meet many other people who are on the same road toward recovery. You will have the benefit of sharing stories and post-op ailments with patients who have had the exact same procedure you have. You may hear yourself saying, "Yes! I'm having that same problem too. I thought it was just me. It's great to hear that it's normal after surgery ..."

Sleep Patterns

It is not unusual to have sleep pattern disruptions after heart surgery. For many heart patients, sleep can become an elusive commodity. The pain associated with trying to find a comfortable sleeping position coupled with suddenly finding oneself sedentary all day can make for many a sleepless night. Some patients may also start to experience "night sweats," even if they never had them before. Eventually, most find that the night sweats go away, but once again, it is another disruption of your regular sleeping pattern.

Some patients stated that it took months before their sleep patterns returned to normal, so be patient. Remember, you need good, solid sleep to help in your healing process. Talk to your doctor and ask about sleep aids, prescription or over-the-counter. Stay on top of your pain medication management; being able to lie comfortably is half the equation.

If you decide to enter cardiac rehab or increase your daily activity, sleep becomes more obtainable. Eventually, your sleep will return to normal and you can finally stop watching all those late-night infomercials.

Special note to potential mechanical heart valve patients: If you search the internet or talk to patients who have had a mechanical heart valve replacement, some will tell you that the clicking noise from the mechanical heart valve opening and closing keeps them awake at night. This clicking can be so loud in some patients that it can be heard by people standing or sleeping next to them. Keep this in mind if you ever have to choose a heart valve and consider yourself very sensitive to noise pollution when trying to fall asleep.

The Miracle Recliner: If you ignore every suggestion offered in this book... and I hope you don't... but if you do... this is the one suggestion many patients will tell you not to ignore: *GET A RECLINER!*

I have had many post-op patients offer this one essential and practical piece of advice: even if you must rent one for your first month home, a recliner is a must for being able to get into a comfortable sitting and sleeping position.

You may soon find upon returning home that lying flat puts enormous pressure and pain on your healing sternum. The distinct change of positions offered by a recliner may ease much of your discomfort.

Be sure the recliner is powered or has an easy-to-pull lever. It may also behoove you to have it delivered and in place *before* you return home; your first few nights will be so much more tolerable and comfortable due to this one preemptive task.

Michele replied to a question about recliners on a heart forum:

Yes, I agree about the recliner. I was able to rent a fully adjustable electric recliner from a medical supply place. I could adjust the foot part and the back part any way I wanted. I did not lie flat for a while afterwards. I had the chair for a month and would ease it back a little more each night until I felt comfortable being almost flat. My incision did give a feeling of being pulled a bit.

*As always, talk to your doctor/surgeon and get his approval to recline in this position postoperatively, especially if you find yourself sleeping for an extended period of time while in the recliner.

Returning to Work

Returning to work is going to be different and unique for each individual. Every job has its various components. Someone who does construction work and heavy lifting will never get back to work before someone who has a more sedentary desk job. However, on average most people can expect to return to work in about eight to 12 weeks.

These restrictions, as you have probably surmised by now, are mainly due to the sternal precautions we have talked so much about throughout this book. However, for many patients who do not have a physical job, mental stress can be just as debilitating. It is not abnormal to have some *mental fog* after heart surgery. This is not to be confused with a very controversial outcome called *pumphead* that is associated with patients who have been placed on the cardio-pulmonary machine.

Pumphead:

I really agonized over whether or not to mention this controversial subject in this book. The intention has always been to ease your anxiety as you prepare for open heart surgery, not add to it. However, I also realize that with the *Internet* at your beck and call, and with many patients thoroughly researching their procedures, it is possible that you may run into this term and phenomenon.

Pumphead is a sort of slang word for the medical term *post-perfusion syndrome*. This is a neurocognitive impairment that may occur from being placed on the cardiopulmonary bypass machine, which takes over your breathing and blood flow.

Neurocognitive impairment?

Yeah, sorry about that — in other words, it means that some people may have deficits in memory, concentration, and attention span after being placed on the cardiopulmonary bypass machine. And although these deficits are usually transient, for some patients they can last for months to years.

There are two main theories as to why this occurs. The first is that when your blood is sent through the tubing on the cardiopulmonary bypass machine, it tends to be temporarily misshapen and thus is unable to efficiently transport oxygenated blood to your brain. The second theory believes that tiny particles of air, organic debris, and thrombus called *microemboli* get into the bloodstream and cause brain ischemia.

However, having said all that, I was recently talking to an anesthesiologist who stated that patients who have had other surgeries not involving the heart or cardiopulmonary bypass have complained of mental deficits postoperatively. This may be caused by the anesthetic gases and paralytic agents used, which can affect the brain.

The bottom line and the thing you must hold on to is that most studies show that the majority of patients who were placed on the heart-lung machine had no significant deterioration in their mental abilities after surgery!

Aside from pumphead, some patients find that after heart surgery their minds are not as sharp as they were before. This mental malaise can linger for months, with some patients claiming they never really returned to their baseline mental sharpness. Add to that the stress of returning to work and having to deal with the mental tasks associated with your job can be just as debilitating as physical constraints.

Be aware of your strengths and weaknesses after your heart surgery. Listen to your doctor when he/she warns you not to be so eager to get back into the "rat race." If your finances and lifestyle allow you more time, take it. If they do not, see if your doctor can give you permission to ease back into work. Start with reduced hours or two days a week. Work into it slowly, that way you can gauge with every work day how you are progressing.

Nuisance Pain

By the time you've hit your fifth week, most of your pain should have abated. However, many patients may still experience "nuisance pain." This is pain that presents more as an irritation rather than as the sharp, debilitating pain you may have felt during weeks one through three.

This pain can present itself anywhere along your incision. Even as far as 16 weeks out, patients have complained about being sore along some portion of their incision. Some describe it as a burning sensation, especially when in contact with their clothing or car seatbelt. Most doctors would probably label this soreness as normal. It is an unfortunate phase of your healing cycle. The nerves surrounding your sternum, ribs, arms, or legs take time to recover fully.

If you had bypass surgery and your surgeon used your left IMA (Internal Mammary Artery) for one of your bypasses, you may find the left side of your chest more sore and sensitive than your right. Patients have complained that weeks to months after their surgeries this left side was still "numb." This numbness becomes irritated when brushed against clothing or, as previous stated, when rubbed against a seatbelt. Although some patients say it still bothers them six months post-surgery, the consensus seems to be that over time this irritation abates and is eventually healed and forgotten. And as one patient reconciled it: *"Hey it hurts, and it's bothersome, but I'm still alive!"*

Although this may be part of your normal healing process, you must still stay vigilant and aware. You are still susceptible to a sternal wound infection so, as stated earlier in this book, watch for fever, redness, swelling, and warmth around your wound. If you have excessive pain around your sternum or if there is leaking fluid or pus, call your doctor immediately. These warnings also apply to any location on your body where you had an incision: your leg, your tube sites, even your arm IV sites.

Also, beware: sometimes the wires used to close your sternum can start to erode through your skin. This erosion may present itself as a sharp point when you feel the area with your hand. In some cases, once your sternum is fully healed, your surgeon will go back and remove one or all your wires.

Chapter 6: Popular Heart Web Forums

My original intention was to end this book with a listing of some websites I believed would help you on your surgical journey. However, there are so many great sites available that I felt the need to expound on each of them to really promote their value.

Heart-Valve-Surgery.com

Heartvalvesurgery.com is such a great site that it deserves the first mention. Founded by Adam Pick in 2006, this site has become the go-to site for not only information about heart surgery, but also for camaraderie and inspiration from other patients. This site has had millions (yes, millions) of viewers and participants and has helped millions of patients through their journeys.

Adam's story is that he urgently needed double heart valve surgery in 2005. He researched the procedure, found a very well-qualified surgeon, and is now living proof of the success of modern-day heart surgery. After recovering, he wrote a book called **The Patient's Guide to Heart Valve Surgery**, now in its seventh edition. This led to his inspiring website, ***www.heartvalvesurgery.com***.

Although his site offers plenty of information about surgical procedures, doctors, hospitals, and recovery strategies, its greatest strength is its "Community" tab. Here is where thousands of people and patients talk and encourage each other through their respective surgeries. Click on *"Success Stories"* and try not to be encouraged and inspired. It is impossible! There you can read about great surgical successes, from average people like Anita to the famous ABC newscaster Barbara Walters. Being able to follow their journeys from diagnosis to finding a surgeon to the operation itself, and of course, to full recovery is awe-inspiring and encouraging. It truly is a community. And although its focus is on heart valve surgery, there are plenty of patients who have had other types of heart surgeries: coronary bypass, aortic aneurysms, and cardiac cauterizations.

The "Learning Center" tab on Adam's web page is extremely helpful in answering questions and allaying fears about symptoms, treatment options, hospital stays, and even recovery expectations. What's great is that Adam not only responds to some of the questions, but patients, doctors, nurses, and surgeons are all present to offer their experiences. I also found the links to videos and seminars to be extremely educational. Actual cardiac surgeons answer patient questions about surgery and recovery. There are also animated videos about all types of heart surgeries. Please visit this site as an adjunct to this book. I promise it will encourage, educate, and inspire you!

Speaking of inspire:

Inspire

If heart-valve-surgery.com is my favorite cardiac website, then *Inspire* has to be my second favorite site. The web page is ***www.inspire.com***. Inspire is an online support group and discussion community. Here you can sign in and talk to thousands of patients who are going through the same illness and difficulties that you may be experiencing. Any disease, any illness, any medication regimens are represented within its support pages and groups. The groups range from diabetes to cancer to genetic disorders; any ailment or disease you can think of is represented. Even groups about health insurance, hospices, and parenting are represented.

However, for our purposes, it is the *Heart Groups* we would most likely visit. I especially enjoy talking in the group *Life After Heart Bypass Surgery*. The people who participate here are kind and encouraging; they support and hearten (no pun intended) each other. It is so encouraging to follow someone's journey from the time they first become a member — scared and frightened about their upcoming surgery — to the triumph of their logging in to tell us it's over and they are back home safe and sound. If you truly want some advice, compassion, and camaraderie, this is the site for you!

Mended Hearts

I love the whole premise of Mended Hearts *(www.mendedhearts.org)*. Let me start by quoting their mission statement:

"Our mission is dedicated to 'Inspiring hope and improving the quality of life for heart patients and their families through ongoing peer-to-peer support.'"

Their homepage states their origins much better than I ever could:

"Mended Hearts is a national and community-based non-profit organization that has been offering the gift of hope to heart disease patients, their families, and caregivers. Founded by Dr. Dwight E. Harken, The Mended Hearts was started with four of Dr. Harken's open heart surgery patients. In January 1951 Dr. Harken asked Doris Silliman, one of the first 50 patients to ever have heart surgery, and three other post-surgery heart patients – Keith Otto, Alford Santimassino and Elizabeth Wilkinson

– to meet at the hospital. They spoke of their new feeling of well-being, their plans, and hopes for the future – and with renewed happiness, they spoke of their "mended hearts." They realized how wonderful it would be to provide support and help others facing the same experience.

"With the assistance of Dr. Harken, they formed an organization, wrote up a charter and planned their membership contacts with the aid of the hospital workers. They called themselves the Mended Hearts. They often spoke of how great it was to be alive and to help others."

The rest is 50-plus years of history and direct patient support. During your hospital stay, you may even be visited by a Mended Heart volunteer. Former cardiac patients volunteer their time to visit patients and their families, offering first-hand knowledgeable support and information.

If you are one of those people who truly believe that all good fortune should be "passed forward," you may want to consider volunteering with Mended Hearts after your recovery. I know of some patients who have volunteered because during their time of anxiety and fret, they were visited and comforted by a Mended Heart volunteer.

Mended Heart also has a great magazine that is offered online. Once on the site, go to the *"Resources"* tab and then click on the ***"Heartbeat Magazine"*** tab. The magazine is bi-monthly and provides valuable articles for the patient. The direct link is **mendedhearts.org/resources/heartbeat-magazine**.

ValveReplacement.org

ValveReplacement .org states that it is "*a heart valve replacement community.*"

It is a community forum/bulletin board where people share their stories and questions about heart surgery. Just as with Heart-Valve Surgery.com, don't be fooled by the name. This forum and its wonderful, supportive members talk about all aspects of heart surgery, as indicated by the first panel you see when you go to their site: *Heart Talk.* Here is where members and visitors discuss all general issues related to heart surgery.

Some other tabs are:

Pre-Surgery area is where members can talk about "*those tense weeks leading to heart surgery.*"

Post Surgery area contains discussions about life after surgery: "*the ups and downs and how it is transitioning back to a normal life.*"

Significant Others Forum is unique in that it is geared toward family members and how they handle all the stress, highlights, and triumphs that arise when taking care of a loved one after surgery. If you are stressed and confused by the recovery process you are enduring with your spouse or family member; this is a great place for insight and empathy.

Other forum areas include:
Active Lifestyles & Cardiac Rehabilitation, Home Anti-Coagulation Monitoring, Recipes for Heart Patients, and New Advances

This is one of the most supportive sites I visit. If you have a pending question, this is the place to ask it and get the answers and support you need.

HealthGrades

A very popular site for finding doctors, surgeons, hospitals, and other healthcare providers is *www.healthgrades.com*. HealthGrades is considered one of the leading online resources for finding comprehensive information about physicians and hospitals. More than one million people a day visit this site to vet hospital and healthcare providers.

HealthGrades' mission statement sums it up best:

"Our mission is to help consumers find the right doctor and the right hospital, for the right care. We provide consumers with the information they need to make more informed decisions, including information about the provider's experience, patient satisfaction, and hospital quality... we are dedicated to delivering solutions that bring a new level of transparency to healthcare."

HealthGrades offers information about hospitals as well as doctors, and it is written in friendly, straightforward, non-technical language. Here you can see the mortality and complication rates of every hospital in the United States. The site also offers patient satisfaction ratings using a five-star system; here patients can state their experiences with doctors as well as office staff. Learn which doctors are *board-certified* and what types of procedures they perform the most. If you are the kind of person who likes to research everything from your doctor to the institution in which he works, this is the website for you. More than three million healthcare providers are listed. This is a great and informative site!

Society of Thoracic Surgery

Another web page you may find helpful is ***www.sts.org***. This is the Society of Thoracic Surgery. Click on the *"Patients"* tab and browse around. There is plenty of good and useful information. They also have links to ratings of surgery groups and hospitals throughout the country. Under that same patient's tab, click on *"Heart Surgery Outcomes — Public Access"* and then *"Adult Cardiac Surgery Database Public Reporting."* It is a bit dry, but they give star ratings to hospitals and cardiac surgery groups.

Conclusion

Thank you again for purchasing this book!

I hope it has helped as you prepare for or recover from your open heart surgery. Wherever you are on this journey— whether you just received your diagnosis or are days away from scheduled surgery, stay strong and focused. Picture yourself reaching your goals for life after open heart surgery: returning to work, enjoying walks with your family, playing sports, going on vacations, or even just resting in your favorite chair and watching TV.

I believe Vicky, a heart forum member, put it best as she wrote to thank her fellow forum members for their support at her one-year anniversary post-CABG (Coronary Artery Bypass Graft):

"One year anniversary of CABG x2. Doing happy dance. Yes, my incision site is still tender, but I am leaving for a trip to Italy in three weeks and have already taken a cruise from Hawaii to Vancouver, BC and [I have also] taken our motor home to North and South Dakota for a two-week holiday. All in the last four months! Thank you, God and all the people that made my continued life possible. Life is a winding road, and I am happy to be on it. We live on and hope for the best. I truly love you all. Take special care and keep on keeping on..."

Vicky

This life is so unpredictable and so full of curves that we need each other just to see it straight. Look to your family, your friends, and, yes, even your healthcare providers. We are all here to see you around the bends.

You are not alone on this journey.

So, when you awake from anesthesia, open your eyes, and look around ... we will all be there keeping you strong.

Good luck and God bless.

P.S. If you enjoyed this book, I'd like to ask you for a favor; would you be kind enough to leave a positive review on Amazon? It would be greatly appreciated!

Please visit our *Facebook* page, **Surgery: Open Heart**, or participate in our group page, **Surgery: Open Heart Groups**. On the group page, you can ask questions and talk to other heart patients about your concerns and fears — and, of course, your triumphs!

Thanks!

Appendix A: Understanding Valve Surgery

If you are reading this section, you most likely have been diagnosed with some type of valvular heart disease. This valve disease can involve one or more of the four valves in your heart: *mitral, tricuspid, aortic, and pulmonary valve.* This disease process could have come about through several avenues; however, it is usually associated with plain old aging. This is referred to as *degenerative valve disease.*

Your heart valves, depending on your standing heart rate, can cycle (open and close) nearly 40 million times a year or more than two billion times in your lifetime. That is a lot of wear and tear on a delicate paper-thin piece of tissue no larger in diameter than a quarter. Their primary function is simple: *allow blood to flow in only one direction within your heart.* In order for this to occur your valves must be properly shaped and supple, open fully so all the blood can pass through them easily, and then close as tight as a drum so blood can't leak backward into the chamber it just exited from.

To understand how a heart valve functions, try to think of it as a swinging saloon door as seen in the old western movies. However, this bar door is unique in that it swings in only one direction, letting people enter the saloon, but not exit. So it is with heart valves — they allow blood to flow in only one direction and not the other. It is when they become faulty that they may allow blood to flow back in the opposite direction (valve regurgitation), or they may limit the amount of blood able to flow at all in its original swing destination (valve stenosis).

Let's start with aortic valve disease since it is a very common valve illness and subsequent operation. Your aortic valve is a three-leaflet valve that allows blood to flow from your main heart chamber, the left ventricle, to your main artery, the aorta. From there blood can be perfused to your entire body. The aortic valve's job is to let that oxygen-rich blood flow out of its chamber, the left ventricle, but not allow any blood to flow back into that chamber. The new blood will enter your heart's chamber through other valves — your mitral valve, to be precise.

When the disease process hits your aortic valve, it either doesn't allow enough blood out of the chamber (stenosis) or once the blood is pumped out of the chamber, the valve does not close completely, allowing blood to leak back into the ventricle chamber (regurgitation or insufficiency). This disease process can be caused by infection, calcifications, tumors, rheumatic fever, aortic dilatation, congenital malformations, or even radiation therapy for another ailment.

Aortic Valve Disease: Regurgitation

Regurgitation is usually discussed when referring to the two main heart valves: the mitral valve and the aortic valve. Let's take a look at the aortic valve first.

Aortic valve regurgitation decreases the pumping efficiency of the heart and limits the amount of blood being pumped to the body. In this analogy, your swinging saloon doors no longer meet and close as tight as a drum; they have a space between them when closed. Because of this, blood leaks backward into your heart chamber, forcing your heart to work harder to push that same blood a second time out of its chamber. Over time this can result in atrial fibrillation and congestive heart failure. Symptoms can range from shortness of breath to severe exhaustion. Extremity swelling is a standard complication of this disease and its related congestive heart failure.

Your doctor may have used the terms *aortic insufficiency* or *aortic incompetence* –in layman's terms, *a leaking heart valve*. He/she may also have determined the degree of insufficiency via an echocardiogram study. Here he/she would have labeled your condition as *mild, moderate, or severe.*

Aortic valve regurgitation *usually* progresses slowly over many years. Statistically, its genesis is most likely from a congenital condition (bicuspid aortic valve), or it may be something as simple as a dental abscess or rheumatic fever as a child. Whatever its origins, patients start to notice that they are becoming more and more short of breath and fatigued upon exertion. They can start to notice heart palpitations as they develop a fluttering heart or atrial fibrillation. Their feet and ankles eventually become swollen as their heart loses its ability to pump blood efficiently throughout their bodies.

Aortic Valve Disease: Stenosis

In aortic stenosis, the leaflets of your valve become abnormally rigid. They do not open properly or fully, causing a narrowing of the valve. Here your saloon doors, which generally swing open easily and widely (allowing several people in at the same time), are so stiff and narrow that only one person can pass through them at a time. As you can imagine, your heart must work extra hard to pump its blood through this narrow opening. This extra work causes your left ventricle to become enlarged and boggy, leading to progressive heart failure.

This aortic stenosis, if not congenital, is an age-related ailment. Over time, calcium is deposited on the leaflets, making them stiff. It is as if someone forgot to oil your saloon doors and they become stiff and squeaky.

It's about this time you say: *"Okay, enough with the saloon door analogies, we get it!"* ... Sorry.

The breakdown of congenital aortic valve disease falls into three main categories. If a patient is less than 30 years of age and needs an aortic valve replacement, he/she possibly has a *unicuspid unicommissural valve or unicuspid acommissural valve*. A normal aortic valve has three leaflets that open and close synchronously. A unicuspid valve develops when these three leaflets fail to separate before birth. The patient is left with a thin opening of a one-leaflet valve that is very prone to early calcification and stenosis. This type of valve disease is very rare and usually presents as a problem before the age of 30; however, it can also manifest as late as 50 years of age. It is present in males four times more often than in females, yet demonstrates itself in only 0.02 percent of the adult population.

The most common cause of aortic stenosis and the main reason for aortic valve disease is a *congenital bicuspid aortic valve*. Here the patient has two working leaflets – much better than the unicuspid patient but still short of the three leaflets that make up a normal aortic valve. Bicuspid aortic valve presents in one to two percent of the adult population and becomes calcified between the ages of 30 to 70 — much earlier than when a typical three-leaflet aortic valve tends to calcify. This means that for every 1000 births, nearly five babies are born with BAV (Bicuspid Aortic Valve). If a patient presents for aortic valve surgery between these ages, he/she most likely has a bicuspid aortic valve.

After age 70, even the best tricuspid aortic valves become susceptible to calcium deposits and their associated stenosis and regurgitation. It is unfortunately written into the primer of old age and is often unavoidable. It is when the calcium deposits become disruptive that surgical intervention is warranted.

Note to those who seek medical accuracy: There is a fourth aortic congenital anomaly called quadricuspid aortic valve. However, its prevalence is only 0.01 percent of the adult population.

The patient with aortic stenosis will have many of the symptoms found in aortic regurgitation: shortness of breath, decreased exercise endurance, chest pain or heaviness, and swelling of the extremities. The patient may also experience heart palpitations and syncope — episodes in which they pass out.

It should be noted that unresolved aortic stenosis/regurgitation can lead to ventricular hypertrophy and an enlarged left atrium. This can become important to the patient choosing between a mechanical or bioprosthetic valve in that an enlarged left atrium can lead to atrial fibrillation. Most patients who have AFib will be placed on a blood thinner – the same blood thinner some patients may be trying to avoid by choosing a bioprosthetic valve over a mechanical valve. We will discuss these choices in detail later.

Bicuspid Aortic Valve Patients and Family Need Constant Monitoring

The most recent studies suggest that bicuspid aortic valve disease may be caused by a congenital connective tissue disorder. Therefore, bicuspid aortic patients must be monitored for life-threatening complications such as abdominal and thoracic aortic aneurysms, aortic dissections, and coronary artery problems. **Those diagnosed with bicuspid aortic valve should be constantly monitored by their physicians for the above stated life-threatening conditions.**

Bicuspid aortic valve and its associated risks are also an inherited condition. If you have been diagnosed with this condition, you should notify family members about their familial genetic susceptibility. Immediate family members as well as extended family members (nephews, nieces, and even grandchildren) should all be screened by their physicians or cardiac specialists for associated diseases.

Aortic Valve Disease: Treatments

The severity of aortic valve disease can sometimes be managed with medications; however, no drug regimen can cure aortic disease. The symptoms can be masked or reduced, but eventually, surgery is the only avenue.

Unfortunately for most patients, the longer they delay surgical intervention, the more irreversible damage they may be doing to their heart. Regrettably, far too many patients *fall off the radar* when they are plagued with a slow but debilitating disease. They are advised to get yearly check-ups and to stay acutely aware of their progressive symptoms, but they either ignore the problem or are too scared of the surgical intervention.

Don't be one of those patients! As you may have figured out by now, the goal of this book is to prepare you for heart surgery, not frighten you. However, right here and now is one of those exceptions!

The facts of several studies state that for individuals with **severe untreated *symptomatic*** aortic stenosis who ignore their symptoms and refuse surgery, the death rate after two years is 50 percent! Whereas, the success rate nationwide for overall valve surgery is over 95 percent.

Easy math, right?

Follow your doctor's recommendations and complete all the monthly or yearly studies he/she prescribes for you. Valve disease, aortic or mitral, can cause long-term processes to occur in your body that may not be reversible. Every center and every cardiologist may have different parameters; however, management and follow-up studies with echocardiograms should reflect something similar to the following:

- **Severe aortic stenosis:** yearly follow-up and echocardiogram

- **Moderate aortic stenosis:** every 3 years follow-up and echo

- **Mild aortic stenosis:** every 5 years follow-up and echo

Aortic valve replacement is eventually the option most patients are forced to choose. Here your surgeon will place you on a heart-lung machine, open your aorta, remove the valve and its surrounding calcium, and place in a new valve —either mechanical, bioprosthetic, or to a lesser degree homograft via the Ross Procedure. All of these options will be covered later in this book when we discuss valve choices. It should be noted that after aortic valve replacement, there is up to a six percent chance that a permanent pacemaker will need to be inserted for persistent complete heart block.

Depending on the statistics one reads, up to 40 percent of patients are too weak or ill to undergo open heart valve repair. For these patients, a non-surgical option has recently come on the horizon called TAVR (TransCatheter Aortic Valve Replacement). This procedure can be done under local anesthesia and is percutaneous for most patients in that no surgical incision is needed to place the aortic valve. Your surgeon can place your heart valve through two punctures in your groin, much like cardiac stenting. This option will also be discussed when we come to valve choices later in the chapter.

Mitral Valve Disease: Regurgitation

In mitral valve regurgitation, the two leaflets of your mitral valve do not seal properly. Frequently, what happens is that these valves get pulled apart and are no longer able to reach each other. As a result of this, blood leaks backward in your heart, forcing your heart to re-pump the blood it had previously tried to pump out of its chamber: your left atrium. Mitral valve disease is considered the most common valvular disease in humanity. Either condition (stenosis or regurgitation) places great strain on your cardiac muscles.

If one of the valves breaks loose and flops "in the breeze," *per se* (but actually back into your left atrium), it is called *mitral valve prolapse*. In my growing, annoying analogy, one door in your pair of saloon doors is literally off its hinge. This congenital condition affects about two to three percent of the population, with more than double the percentage being women. In *most cases* mitral valve prolapse is harmless. *

However, please see the warning in the vignette below.

97

Individuals may walk around unaware that they have it until a heart murmur is found on examination or the prolapse becomes severe. These patients may eventually complain of rapid heartbeats (palpitations), fatigue, or some type of chest discomfort. It is now when your doctor may schedule you for an echocardiogram or an MRI, depending on your circumstances.

This regurgitation is also referred to as *mitral incompetence* or *mitral insufficiency*. Many patients refer to it as *"a leaking heart."* No matter how it is labeled, mitral valve regurgitation, for the most part, is a slowly progressive disease. It is graded on a scale of one to four (mild, moderate, moderately severe, or severe) where four (severe) is the worst. On the lower end of the scale (mild), your cardiologist may simply watch and keep an eye on your valves' condition. Conversely, once a patient gets to four out of four, it is considered severe and must be addressed immediately.

There are generally two spectrums of degenerative mitral valve diseases: *Barlow's disease* to *fibroelastic deficiency*, with varying abnormalities between the two ranges.

In Barlow's disease, the leaflets are large and thickened, with a large annular size. Its occurrence is in the patient who has had a lengthy history of a heart murmur and is younger than 60 years old when symptoms start to develop.

At the other end of the spectrum is fibroelastic deficiency, a degenerative heart disease in patients over the age of 60 who have an annulus usually normal in size and a short history of heart murmurs. These patients tend to have a shorter record of valve regurgitation and may present with a single chord rupture.

> **A Warning to Patients:** Although mitral valve disease usually takes years to progress in severity, and in its early stages can be asymptomatic (showing no ill effects from the disease), in some patients it can go from moderate to severe in the course of just a few months, especially in cases of mitral valve prolapse. If you have been diagnosed with a heart murmur or some type of mitral valve degenerative disease, it is imperative that you have regular checkups with your doctor or cardiologist. If left unchecked and unmonitored, mitral valve disease can be extremely detrimental to one's health, even fatal.

The symptoms of mitral valve regurgitation are somewhat similar to those of aortic valve disease: fatigue when exercising or exerting, heart palpitations, and a cough at bedtime. However, shortness of breath when lying down is the key marker for mitral regurgitation. It is the blood leaking from the left ventricle, backward through the mitral valve, and eventually back into the lungs causing shortness of breath. Long-standing mitral regurgitation can lead to atrial fibrillation and even end up as *congestive heart failure*. This is where the heart is not able to pump enough blood to meet your body's needs.

Mitral Valve Disease: Stenosis

Sticking with our saloon door analogy ... *you thought it was gone, didn't ya* ... when you have mitral valve stenosis, your saloon doors become stiff (calcified) and no longer easily open all the way. It is as if your hinges have become old and rusty and it takes great effort to push those doors open. In mitral valve stenosis, there is a narrowing of the mitral valve from the valves not being able to open completely. The valve becomes thickened and calcified. Where mitral valve regurgitation occurs over time with age, mitral stenosis can be the result of rheumatic fever as a child. It can also be the result of an infection caused by bacteria that have the propensity to attach to the mitral valve. Other causes include high blood pressure and coronary artery disease.

The symptoms of mitral valve stenosis are very similar to those listed above in the regurgitation section. However, the bigger risk with stenosis is the threat of an enlarged heart due to the excessive work the heart must endure pumping blood out of its left atrial chamber.

As in mitral regurgitation, a patient may have mild symptoms for years. However, with stenosis, a patient can be completely asymptomatic even with severe disease. Many times, the condition is picked up during a regular physical when the doctor hears an abnormal heart sound through his/her stethoscope.

Rheumatic fever is the leading cause of mitral valve stenosis. Most often a patient (as a child) starts with strep throat and then develops rheumatic fever, which leads to scarring on the mitral valve as well as other heart conditions.

Mitral Valve Disease: Treatments

Once again, there isn't any effective medical therapy that will cure mitral valve stenosis. Moreover, many patients with mitral regurgitation can remain asymptomatic (having no ill effects of their disease) for extended periods of time. Your doctor may prescribe medication that can ease your symptoms and aid in your heart's function. If your ailment is mitral valve regurgitation, there may not be an urgency for surgical intervention. Many doctors closely monitor these patients and offer medical therapy (beta blockers or ACE inhibitors) until the patients become severely symptomatic. Recent studies, however, show that it may be more beneficial to operate on asymptomatic mitral-valve-diseased patients rather than monitor and wait. There is a growing argument that it is best to have surgery prior to the onset of any left ventricular dysfunction. It all depends on your physical condition and debilitation, or on what you and your doctor determine is the appropriate form of intervention.

The options available for stenosis are mitral valve repair, replacement, or balloon valvuloplasty. As stated earlier, the mitral valve is the most commonly repaired valve in your heart. If your surgeon can repair it, he/she may opt for that avenue over mitral valve replacement. Recent studies have shown the benefit of mitral valve repair over mitral valve replacement in patients with degenerative mitral regurgitation. These studies noted that patients who had repairs displayed fewer post-op complications, better survival statistics, and fewer valve-related complications. And although some of these studies were not a "randomized control study" and thus has the potential to be skewed and biased, the results were quite noteworthy with respect to the 20-year survival rate. Patients with mitral valve repairs had a survival rate that was nearly double that of the replacement group. *As always stated: This is a small synopsis of a very large study. Every patient is unique, so you should consult thoroughly with your doctor on the correct procedure and surgical route you should undertake.*

In many cases, the mitral valve can be repaired with a high incidence of success. Your surgeon will reconstruct the native valve tissues to restore them back to their original structure and return them to their original function. Out of all the valves in your heart, this is the most commonly repaired valve as compared to replacements. A surgical repair also preserves the integrity of the left ventricle's structure. If the valve cannot be repaired, your surgeon must replace it. This scenario tends to occur more frequently in patients who have had a previous heart attack.

If the surgeon cannot repair your mitral valve, he/she will opt for replacement. He/she may even attempt a repair at first and then, while judging its results, replace the valve moments later. Mitral valve surgery and reconstruction are complex tasks. Of all the cardiac procedures done in America, valve surgery is considered the most technically challenging. Remember, as in any field, there are experts and those renowned for their achievements. Mitral valve repair falls under this category. Ask your cardiologist who is the best. Depending on your disease process, he/she may refer you to a *reference mitral valve surgeon*. This is a specialist in mitral valve repair. These surgeons can boast repair success rates in the high 90 to 100 percent range and they have performed hundreds of successful mitral valve repairs. If you are told that the chances of a successful repair rate are below 60 percent or if you have a complex mitral valve, such as Barlow's valve, it may behoove you to seek a *reference mitral valve surgeon*. It may involve some travel, but in the end, it will likely be worth the effort.

It's not that you wouldn't seek the best surgeon for any surgery, but it's here where you want to do your *due diligence*. Find a center and surgeon who specializes in valve surgery. Ask how many valves he/she does a year and what is his/her success rate and mortality/stroke rate. You don't want a cardiac surgeon or center that does heart bypasses and an occasional valve; you want a center that does more than 300 valve procedures a year with a success rate in the high 90s.

Non-Invasive Mitral Valve Procedure

Since 2013, patients have had the option, when appropriate, to have a non-surgical mitral valve repair from a transcatheter device called a *MitraClip*. As in the case with TAVR or cardiac stents, this device can be placed from a catheter stick in your groin; no cutting of the sternum or ribs is needed to gain access to your heart and mitral valve. Again, as in early TAVR patients, this procedure is usually reserved for those patients who are deemed too sick to survive an open-heart valve replacement. MitraClip is most effective on patients with functional or degenerative mitral regurgitation.

A one-year study (according to *Abbott Vascular*) of approximately 3,000 high-surgical-risk patients showed that patients who had received the MitraClip had "significant improvements." Nearly 93 percent of the patients had a significant downgrade of their mitral regurgitation and 80 percent of patients remained free from re-hospitalization one year after implantation.

Appendix B: Choosing the Right Heart Valve

Okay. You've come to accept the fact that you need a heart valve operation. Most likely mitral or aortic valve since they make up the majority of valve replacement operations. You sit down with your cardiologist or your surgeon and he states that *you* must decide whether to receive an artificial mechanical valve or a valve made from pig or cow tissue (bioprosthetic).

Whoa, wait! You mean I have to decide? Aren't you the doctor!?

Yes he is, but in many circumstances the choice becomes yours. It all comes down to lifestyle. And unfortunately, with the advent of a new advanced third option called TAVR (Transcatheter Aortic Valve Replacement), the decision is now even harder. However, before I complicate this situation more, let's see if I can break it down and hopefully clear these muddy waters. Let's start by separating the two main valve choices (mechanical and bioprosthetic) and then finish with how the new technology of transcatheter valve replacement is influencing future valve options.

Mechanical Heart Valves

Mechanical heart valves do not contain any human or animal tissue in their makeup. Most mechanical valves are manufactured using pyrolytic carbon, which is a technical term meaning it's made of crystallized graphite. This graphite material works very well when placed in the human body. There are no adverse reactions initiated from its placement; it is extremely durable and reliable, and it **resists** blood clotting that may form on it. Try to think of it as a comparison between a Teflon cooking pan versus a traditional metal frying pan. Scramble some eggs in the Teflon pan with no oil and they literally slide off, whereas in the metal pan with no oil, the eggs stick all over.

You do not want blood clots sticking to your mechanical valve, for eventually they will break off and lodge somewhere else in your body, possibly giving you a stroke or an embolic event to your heart or lungs. Hence, you want this graphite material on your valve, for not only (like the Teflon pan) is it clot **resistant**, it also has the ability to last a very long time.

In other words, it can last inside your heart in some cases over 30 years.

Now, this is where you need to pay attention because this is the dilemma between the valve choices you may be asked to make.

A 30-year *mechanical valve* means, in most cases, you will not need a second heart operation to replace that valve any time in your lifetime. This is great because a second open heart surgery has a significantly higher morbidity and mortality rate than a first-time open heart operation.

Heads up: *You're going to find out below that your other choice, the bioprosthetic valve, has a finite lifespan of typically only 10 to 15 years!*

Now, you may be saying: *"Okay, stop right there; it's a no-brainer! A 30-year durable, mechanical, non-clotting, Teflon-like valve over a pig or cow valve that lasts only*

10 or so years — I'll take the mechanical valve, thank you very much!"

I truly wish it were that easy. However, the mechanical valve comes with one caveat — one major caveat.

In order to keep that mechanical valve functioning properly and to prevent blood clots from forming on it (remember, I said it was *blood clot resistant*, not blood clot proof), you must take a blood thinner medication... *for the rest of your life.*

The problem is that no matter how well the valve is designed or how Teflon-like the material is, your body still sees the valve as a foreign material. Add to that the fact that the valve's sleek design causes blood shearing, which simply means your blood cells and platelets can become damaged from flowing through the valve. This high shearing of cells and platelets initiates the coagulation cascade, a response that will ultimately lead to the formation of blood clots on the artificial valve leaflets — thus, the reason for taking a blood thinner.

Blood thinner is a layman's term. What you would actually be taking is an anticoagulant. What this drug, most likely Coumadin (Warfarin), does is prevent part of the clotting process that takes place in your body.

When you receive a cut, a dynamic series of events (a cascade) takes place to stop that cut from bleeding. This process starts to form *blood clots*. However, here in this situation, you want blood clots to form to stop your cut from bleeding. What you do not want is for this same cascade series to form clots on your newly placed mechanical heart valve. Coumadin interferes with this clotting process, thus *"thinning your blood"* and making it harder for clots to form on your new mechanical valve.

Now, don't worry; when you do have trauma or cuts, you will indeed stop bleeding, just not as quickly as before.

Unfortunately, when a person is on a blood thinner, they are at risk of having bleeding events. And although these events are rare, they can at times be fatal. Patients on bloodthinners must also pay very close attention to normal lifestyle events such as cuts, bruising, and contact sports. Such events can cause bleeding or hematomas which, although not life-threatening, can cause excessive blood loss and the need for medical intervention.

Also, if you are female and still fertile, the problem becomes even more complicated. Pregnancy and blood thinners are contraindicated. If you plan on having a baby in the future, this is a strong discussion you must have with your doctor. Fortunately, it is rare to have valve replacement needs in patients in their 20s or 30s.

The second problem in receiving a mechanical valve is that these blood thinners you are placed on are somewhat difficult to regulate. Therapeutic blood thinning levels for mechanical valve patients are hard to maintain. Expect to visit a lab to have your blood drawn at least once a month and sometimes as often as twice weekly if you are having trouble regulating your levels. Once the results are read, your doctor will adjust your Coumadin dosage accordingly.

If your clotting time is too long, he/she will lower your dosage; too short and he/she will increase your dosage. It is a delicate balance and statistically your bleeding risk can be four times greater than patients with a *bioprosthetic valve* — who, as you are about to find out, do not need to be on blood thinners.

The goal of being on blood thinners is to decrease the clotting properties of your blood, thus preventing clots from forming on your heart valve. On the other hand, we don't want to keep you from ever clotting; if that were the case, every cut or shaving nick would be a disaster.

Furthermore, as you age, your bleeding risks increase. Once you are past the age of 60, your bleeding risks can increase sevenfold. Also, you will need to notify your doctor or dentist before any procedures that may involve bleeding. This may require some temporary adjustments or bridging of your anticoagulation medications. *(Bridging is temporarily stopping your anticoagulation medicine for several days while placing you on a short acting anticoagulant prior to your procedure; this short acting anticoagulant doesn't last therapeutically long in your body and is usually easily reversed with another drug).*

Moreover, if you have a history of bleeding stomach ulcers, you may not even be a candidate for Coumadin.

Coumadin is a vitamin K antagonist; it works by blocking the formation of vitamin K clotting factors. Your body needs vitamin K to form blood clots and stop bleedings, so expect to endure dietary changes to maintain your body's vitamin K levels. Your doctor will want you to eat the same amount of food at each meal with limiting variance in your green vegetables and other sources of vitamin K. Keeping your vitamin K levels constant is one important step in keeping your INR levels therapeutic.

Tracy from our Facebook Surgery Open Heart Group page writes:

I am one month post-op with a mechanical valve. I take 5 mg of Warfarin (Coumadin) at 6 pm daily. I haven't really noticed a change in diet except keeping away from cranberry juice and too many green leafy vegetables. I believe it was the right choice for me. I am getting use to things day by day.

Now, you may have done your research and noticed that there are home INR/PT Coumadin level tests available to the consumer.

These tests are very similar to home diabetes test machines; you prick your finger with a lancet, place a drop of blood on a test strip, and place it in your machine. With these tests, you save time and needle sticks by not having to visit the lab or your doctor's office to get your blood drawn and your Coumadin levels adjusted.

Right now there seem to be three main companies that provide home testing. In most situations, the home tests, strips, and lancets are reimbursed by Medicare.

My only warning is: if you are going to let these home tests influence your decision regarding a mechanical valve, be sure to have a long discussion with your doctor on their accuracy. There is still considerable debate on their correctness and reliability. Also, go to those web forums I listed in Chapter 6 and search for the terms *Coumadin home kits* or *INR home tests*. See what others who have used the kits are saying; it is very enlightening.

ValveReplacement.org has an entire section that discusses these devices and their results, called *Home Anticoagulation Monitoring*.

A heart forum patient writes on home testing and Coumadin:

The "risks with Coumadin" are few IF you take it as prescribed and routinely test...and with home self-testing, it is a ten-minute test that is done about once per week or so; much like what diabetics do several times a day. I've been on it for 48+ years, and the ONLY problem I've had was due to my ignorance back in the "olden days" (1970's) when knowledge of managing the drug was very limited. If my choice was between Coumadin or future surgeries, I choose mechanical hands down.

I know the aforementioned information may have come across as quite negative. However, these are the lifestyle changes that may need to be addressed when receiving a mechanical heart valve. Conversely, Coumadin is one of the most frequently prescribed drugs in the world. Tens of millions of people take this drug daily, and for most, it is nothing more than a slight nuisance – not something that has taken over their existence. Everyone is different, however, and this is something you must decide along with your doctor and possibly your family. Your decision becomes much easier if you are already on a blood thinner because of a medical condition. Most patients who have atrial fibrillation (AFib) or some thrombotic disorder may already be on a blood thinner, thus making the decision easier.

Now, to reiterate how I started this section: *this valve will most likely last your entire life! You are about to find out in the next section, a bioprosthetic (pig or bovine) valve has a life span of about 10 to 15 years. This means if you are in your 60's or younger you will most likely need another heart operation and valve replacement at some time in your life.*

The guidelines vary from institute to institute, and each surgeon has his/her own parameter that he/she offers his/her patients; however, if you are 70 years or older a bioprosthetic valve will generally last 15 to 20 years. If you are younger than 60, it will most likely last only about 10 years. Thus, the general recommendations are for patients younger than 60 to 65 is to receive a mechanical valve. For patients older than 60 to 65, the recommendation is usually a bioprosthetic valve. For patients aged 60 to 65, both valves are acceptable. What it really comes down to in these situations is the life expectancy of the patient in relation to the valve placed inside him. *Will he/she outlive their valve?*

Once these age criteria are explored and decided on, the patient must consider his/her lifestyle expectations:

- *Am I the type of person who can handle the daily expectations of being on a blood-thinning medicine for the rest of my life? Am I disciplined enough to keep on top of my lab levels? Anticoagulation therapy requires compliance and great discipline!*

- *Do I want a reoperation and recovery every 10 to 15 years?*

- *And what about advancing technology? I could get a biological valve today and then depend on emerging surgical technology and medicine to save me from reoperations, i.e., TAVR, TMVR and MitraClip technology.*

This is something that must be taken into consideration. The reoperation risk is a very serious issue that should not be taken lightly. Your lifetime risk of a reoperation with the bioprosthetic valve can be greater than 25 percent, while your mechanical valve reoperation risk can be lower than four percent, usually due to endocarditis, paravalvular leak, pannus obstruction, or endocarditis. A redo valve operation can be far more risky and complicated than a first-time heart operation. Add to that a prior CABG (coronary artery bypass graft) and your morbidity and mortality rate increases significantly with a second heart operation.

A major factor you may want to discuss with your doctor is *long/short-term survival rates.* Studies vary, but the questions remain the same:

- *Early mortality rates between the two valves; are they similar?*

- *What are the long-term survival rates between mechanical and bioprosthetic valves?*

- *In younger patients, those below 65 years of age, are survival rates better depending on the valve choice?*

- *Does my age affect the mortality rate as it corresponds to my valve choice?*

- *Do my co-morbidities affect the valve options? If I need a bypass or aneurysm repair as well, should that affect my choice in valves?*

Click Click Click: If you remember the section *Sleep Patterns,* we discussed the fact that mechanical valves make an audible clicking sound. This is not a small subject, and for a number of people it is a major deciding factor against the mechanical valve. For some, it is a sleeping problem, while for others, it just freaks them out to hear every stroke of their heart constantly. And yet for many, it is a "non-issue."

Give this subject some thought and due diligence. If you think it's something that could potentially bother you, research it on the forums listed in this book. Not everyone hears a clicking sound. It depends on your anatomy and your valve location. Talk to your doctor; some valves such as the *On-X Plus* are designed to be quieter than others.

From most of my reading and research, it seems most people adjust to the sound over time and eventually never notice it. It's like living by the ocean... eventually you don't hear the waves anymore.

Biological Valves

Bioprosthetic valves are made from either pig (porcine valve) or cow (bovine pericardial valve). If your valve is from a pig, it is the pig's actual valve; if it comes from a cow, it is made from the cow's pericardium (the sac surrounding the cow's heart). A Dacron cuff is usually placed around the valve to give the surgeon an anchor with which to sew the valve into your heart.

As stated earlier, the main advantage of using a bioprosthetic valve is that the patient does not need to be on a lifetime regimen of Coumadin or an equivalent blood thinner. For most of these patients, a daily baby aspirin is all that is required. Your doctor will determine what is best for your situation.

Now, I'm going to reiterate some facts, so please bear with me. It is important that you have a clear understanding of the consequences of your two choices.

The offset of having a bioprosthetic valve is that although you do not have to be on a life-long blood thinner, your valve's duration is curtailed significantly – good for only 10 to 15 years, less if you are younger. This valve is made of biological tissue and the same calcium and lipid deposits that may have hindered your original valve will once again start compromising and degenerating your new valve. And although modern valves are treated with an anti-calcium substance that helps thwart calcium deposits, valve deterioration can begin in less than six years after implantation!

Okay, so I will get this valve, not be on a blood thinner, and take my chances 10 to 15 years from now. Seems like a long time, right?

113

Does it? Time has a way of speeding up the older one gets. Think of the Twin Towers. To me, it seems like only yesterday, but in actuality, it was 15 years ago!

Moreover, one must remember that heart surgery is big surgery. A reoperation of your heart comes with many inherent risks, more so than from the original operation. Also, if you do need a reoperation 15 years later, you are thus 15 years older. And your morbidity and recovery can be directly linked to this increased age.

So, what am I to do?

If your valve problem is mitral, then there is a good chance you surgeon may be able to repair your original valve; then all this discourse will be for not. However, if either valve (aortic or mitral) must be replaced then all you just read is the first step in making your decisions.

Listen carefully to your cardiologist and surgeon. Talk to your family and loved ones. Go to those websites listed earlier and talk to patients who have already experienced what you are deciding. *Inspire.com* is a great sounding board for situations just like this. Look at the new research coming out on mechanical valves. The *On-X Plus Mechanical Valve* now on the market advertises that it needs less blood thinning than the standard traditional mechanical valve. This means for the patient a reduction in the bleeding rate of more than 50 percent while on a lower anticoagulation regimen. One patient on the heart forums stated:

I started out thinking tissue...glad I chose an On-X mechanical. Just past three years post surgery. It sounds and looks great. Coumadin no problem...my range is 1.8 to 2.2. I self-test at home every two weeks with the CoaguChek XS meter. Life is good!

Another patient wrote:

I am 52 and had an AVR done in July...chose mechanical...was right for me. I wasn't worried about Warfarin (Coumadin) [and] preferred not to have another op in future unless something goes badly wrong...I don't think there is a good or bad choice...only what you are comfortable with...I had no idea I had a problem. But three months post op I have never felt so good in [the] last 10 to 15 years.

Andy wrote on a forum also in favor of mechanical valves:

I was 48 years old when I had a mechanical valve for aortic stenosis in something of an urgent situation. I work full time but am not especially sporty, so the prospect of being on Warfarin/Coumadin was not especially concerning and, for me, was a much more attractive option than repeat surgery with a tissue valve. I am diabetic too, and so [I was] used to finger-prick blood tests to monitor blood glucose levels and made a point of getting an INR meter almost immediately so that I can self-test at home/when travelling. I don't like ticking things, and deliberately don't have any ticking clocks or watches, and I hardly notice the ticking of the valve

Chris, another forum member, tried a bioprosthetic aortic valve, but 10 years later had a mechanical valve placed in his heart:

I was pretty bummed too. I had my second AVR in 2011, was 44 at the time, my tissue valve failed after ten years – so, similar boat. In my case, the valve broke one day, and then my chest had a very pronounced vibration – like a blown bearing – the rest of me was behaving a little bit strange too. Calcification hardened the leaflets, and then one of them cracked. So, for me, 2nd time, no research –

surgeon said On-X, I said ok. Afterward, he said he hopes to never see me again. It was a bit of work getting the tissue valve out – well over 2 hours – an awfully long time to have your heart and lungs stopped. For me, the tissue valve didn't really work out, and it wasn't working 100 percent after about year seven, even though the ultrasounds were ok.

So, I've got four years into this On-X valve and so far, so good – actually, it is a noticeable improvement over the last few years of the tissue valve. The Warfarin is not a big deal, but it did mean an extra day in the hospital to sort that out.

I don't restrict my activities; I just have to tell a new massage therapist that the ticking is me. And it doesn't affect my sleeping, which was my worry back then.

The process of deciding which valve is best for you is complex. Each individual will naturally have his/her own criteria and lifestyle to consider. Talk to your cardiologist; he/she should have algorithmic charts or "decision trees" you can look at that help detail the consequences and give you a visual flow-path to some of the basic decisions.

> **Such a Hard Decision:** I recently asked a fellow nurse why her surgical case was delayed. It was a good 45 minutes after her open-heart case was scheduled to begin.
>
> She told me that the surgeon was talking to the patient and the patient was still indecisive as to whether to get a mechanical valve or a bioprosthetic valve. I exclaimed (quietly, I was in the pre-op area), *"How could he have not decided by now?!"*
>
> She raised her shoulders and said she was just as baffled. But it just goes to show how hard of a decision this can be.
>
> *What valve did he finally choose?*
>
> I wish I could tell you. However, I had my own surgical cases to rush off to and like life usually is in a hustling O.R., I was so busy I never remembered to ask the outcome of his dilemma.

For some patients, the algorithm is straightforward:

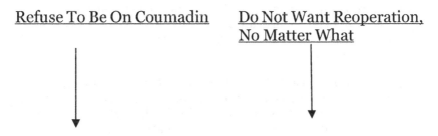

Refuse To Be On Coumadin

Bioprosthetic Valve

Do Not Want Reoperation, No Matter What

Mechanical Valve

It is when the patient's preferences are uncertain that the decision becomes complex. This decision is not unlike what women must go through when dealing with breast cancer; they may have to choose the radical route of mastectomy versus the more conservative lumpectomy.

Unfortunately, life has its own curve balls and no matter what valve you choose, mechanical or bioprosthetic; you may still need a reoperation. Other valves (tricuspid, pulmonary) may fail in the future, or coronary artery disease may set in, each causing you to have that reoperation you were so desperate to avoid.

New Modern Thinking: While writing these chapters on valve choices, I noticed that one of the surgeons I work with was placing a **bioprosthetic aortic valve** in a patient in his mid 50s. Of course, being in the midst of these valve choice writings, I had to run to his room and find out why.

Shouldn't someone so young be getting a mechanical valve?

He explained to me that many younger patients were opting for bioprosthetic valves especially when it came to aortic valve replacements, and he agreed with their thinking. He felt that the morbidity and mortality rates between a primary aortic valve replacement and a secondary aortic valve replacement 15 years later were about the same, with the one caveat being that the primary surgery was just an aortic valve replacement with no other associated surgeries such as bypasses or other valve replacements.

The American Heart Association and American College of Cardiology tend to agree with this thinking. In a 2015 article, they state that as long as the second operation is "done electively in an experienced valve center", most young patients who choose a tissue valve can expect a low operative mortality.

However, as always stated in this book, the above is just a synopsis of a long and complicated study. Do not take the above as gospel. Talk to your doctor, mention the recommendations, and get his input on its results. Studies, as well as their interpretations by both the reader and the writer, can be complicated and skewed toward known biases.

An E.R. nurse who had two previous heart surgeries and who was facing a mitral valve replacement wrote the following on one of the heart forums as she, too, wrestled with the valve choice options:

December 11th, 2015

Looking at MVR in Jan. I'm 43 and have had two previous open heart surgeries. I assumed that due to my surgeries and age I would be given a mechanical valve with no other option. When I sat down with my surgeon, he went over both bioprosthetic tissue valves and mechanical valves and told me that he feels it is a 50/50 decision on which way to go. He gave me info about anticoagulant therapy, lifestyle changes and the risk of strokes if I go mechanical and then the risk of reoperation in 10+ years if I go with the bioprosthetic tissue valve.

He also believes that a reoperation will be low as mitral valve replacements via catheter will be happening in the next few years. I am an ER nurse [and] have a lot of cardiac experience. Coumadin is not a drug that I care to be on; the risk of strokes involved and the possibility of the clicking valve makes mechanical less appealing. But not knowing what the future may bring and possibly having another surgery in 10 years is also not appealing. I really do feel it is a 50/50 split choice considering my history, my lifestyle and knowledge of medicine after talking with my doctor and his staff. I sort of wish he wouldn't have given me an option. I had resigned myself [to the fact] that [it] wasn't an option and [I] was going to have to do what I have to do and get mechanical and just deal with it. Now...I'm more confused than ever.

After much consideration and soul-searching, she finally opted for the mechanical valve.

* *It should be noted that her choice was predicated on other personal medical factors not represented in this one portion of her conversation.*

I thank her for allowing me to share her struggles and story!

Ross Procedure

Okay, so maybe you're one of those people who says: *"Hey, I don't think I like any of those options! I don't want to be on a blood thinner, and I sure as hell don't want to go through open heart surgery twice, let alone three times! I want a third option!"*

In that case, let me introduce you to Dr. Donald Ross, the pioneer of the Ross procedure, first performed in 1967. The Ross procedure, sometimes called a *Switch Procedure*, takes the heart's pulmonary valve and places (switches) it in the aortic position, making the pulmonary valve your new aortic valve. The major advantage of this operation is that you are placing a living valve into your aorta. (Remember, your bioprosthetic valve, though tissue is not *live tissue* and your mechanical valve is a *synthetic material*.) In this position, your pulmonary valve will communicate with its surrounding tissue, grow new cells, and be able to grow in size as your body grows (granted, if placed during your growing years). It will not be vulnerable to tissue rejection and overt calcium attraction. This is your own body's valve. Statistically, it offers better flow ratios than bioprosthetic valves and can last in patients well past 20 years in this position. There is no need to be on blood thinners your entire life. Because it is a living valve, it will also have a lower thrombogenicity factor (clots will not form on it) and a greater resistance to infections and its associated endocarditis.

Whoa, wait a minute! This sounds great! Why didn't you mention this before all the other valve choices? I'm in!

Before you get too excited, there are a few caveats that really need to be addressed. First of all, you now no longer have a pulmonary valve; we removed it and gave it to your aorta, so you now need a pulmonary valve.

Your pulmonary valve position would then be replaced with a homograft, also called an allograft. This would be a human valve from a cadaver donor. *Many patients ask, "Why not just put the homograft in the aortic position right from the start and not have to switch two valves?"*

The left side of your heart that your aortic valve works in is considered a high-pressure system and the right side of your heart is a low-pressure system. Your aortic valve works a lot harder than your pulmonary valve. A homograft in this aortic position would not last as long in this high-pressure system. The other problem is that homografts do not have statistical longevity; they too are prone to calcium deposits and other biological problems – although it is human cadaver valve, it is not live tissue.

One of the other caveats: studies going as far back as 20 years show a high reoperation rate for Ross procedure patients, mainly due to the dilation of the aorta and pulmonary valve in the aortic position. Furthermore, this is a very complex operation, and it requires an extremely skilled cardiac surgeon to perform the surgery. It is also a *two-valve* operation and the coronary arteries (the arteries that supply blood to your heart) must be removed and then re-implanted in most cases. Critics of this procedure are quick to point out that the patient is trading a single-valve disease for a double-valve disease by nature of this two-valve operation. And even when successfully performed, post-operatively the patient's blood pressure must be closely monitored and controlled for up to six months while all the implanted tissues take root.

Enthusiasm for the Ross Procedure has waxed and waned since 1967 when it was first introduced. According to the Society of Thoracic Surgeon's Cardiac Database, Ross Procedures peaked in 1998 to around 1.2 percent of all aortic valve procedures in the United States, then steadily declined from there to around 0.2 percent in 2006 and .09 percent in 2010. Today the Ross Procedure accounts for only two to three percent of all aortic valve replacements *worldwide.*

If you think carefully about those statistics, it means that 97 percent of surgeons and cardiologists in the world believe it is better for their patients to receive the traditional bioprosthetic or mechanical aortic valve!

Mechanical valve replacement in patients middle-aged and younger is still the most often performed aortic valve replacement. Furthermore, studies show that the Ross Procedure performs best for patients with *aortic stenosis* versus those who have *aortic regurgitation.*

So now that I have dampened your enthusiasm – what's the bottom line?

The Ross Procedure, though controversial, is a definitely an alternative for aortic valve replacement, especially in the patient 50 to 60 years of age and younger. This is provided that said patient has limited cardiac or medical co-morbidities. At this time, there seems to be no magic age at which the Ross Procedure is no longer a viable avenue; however, the further away from the age of 50 you are, the lesser the chance of your surgeon being enthusiastic about its viability.

Those surgeons who perform the Ross Procedure are great proponents of its validity and success; those who don't will espouse that mechanical and bioprosthetic aortic valve replacements are definitely the *Gold Standard* in the 21st century. Talk to your cardiologist and your surgeon; each patient's criteria and circumstances will naturally dictate the answer – *but so will your doctor's personal opinion about the Ross Procedure.* Don't be surprised if your physician is not an advocate; there is a very small subgroup that promotes this procedure in today's medical world. Remember, this is a highly complex procedure and it should be performed only by those who are highly skilled in its operation. If this is your path, choose a surgeon who has done several Ross Procedures, preferably in the 50 to 300 range. This is a very complicated procedure and you want someone who has been performing it for decades and who has great results. You also want it performed in a hospital that has a long history of Ross experience. Patients after a Ross Procedure need life-long measurable follow-ups to monitor for autograph dilations and regurgitation. Echocardiograms and tomography must be performed by specialists who possess acute knowledge of Ross Procedures and their associated complications. Patients should be entered into a Ross database and monitored for follow-up non-compliance.

Several studies confirm that the risks of this operation are surgeon-dependent. However, in the hands of an experienced Ross surgeon and in a hospital with years of Ross experience, this operation can be an avenue other than the mechanical or bioprosthetic valve. In your search, you will quickly discover (with the exception of pediatric and very young patients) that centers offering Ross Procedures are scarce throughout the country, if not the world.

John from *Facebook Ross Procedure Support Network* writes to a fellow member who is getting "a little nervous" about her upcoming Ross Procedure:

I recall my own feelings getting the Ross many years ago, saying goodbye to my little boys as I headed to Salt Lake City. You will be surprised at the calmness that will hit you as you actually get to the hospital and prep for the procedure. What you need to remember is that you will go to sleep and you WILL wake up – and it will be done. Your job is simple: recover and get out of that bed ASAP and start walking. All will be well, my young friend; God isn't done with you yet!

TAVR (Transcatheter Aortic Valve Replacement)

As alluded to earlier, TAVR has muddied the waters just a bit more when it comes to the aortic heart valve decision for future patients. This type of surgery (FDA approved in 2011) is minimally invasive, meaning it can usually be performed under local anesthetic and without making an incision in the patient. There may also be no need for that dreaded neck IV (Swan catheter) or Foley catheter discussed in chapter 2. This modern procedure replaces and repairs your aortic valve without removing your failing old valve.

Your surgeon, along with a team of Interventional Cardiologists, makes a small puncture in your groin, accessing your femoral artery. From that access point, they can place a fully collapsed valve (strategically placed on a catheter) all the way up your femoral artery, into your aortic arch, and finally in your heart, right where your original aortic valve lies. Once in position, the valve is deployed from its catheter and expanded (opened) in your aorta, replacing your damaged valve. Actually, it pushes your old valve against the aorta and takes over its place and function. (Think of a collapsed umbrella as the valve on the catheter and the open umbrella as the valve is deployed.)

The reason this is a new factor in your decision between a mechanical aortic valve and a bioprosthetic aortic valve is the following: some patients (not all) are opting for the bioprosthetic valve over the mechanical valve in the hopes that 10 to 15 years down the road when their bioprosthetic aortic valve fails, this new technology will be in place. At that time they can then get a new aortic valve without major open heart surgery.

Are they right? That is a question you must ask your doctor if this becomes a part of your decision tree.

The *Annals of Thoracic Surgery* reported this year that middle-aged patients are increasingly choosing bioprosthetic valves as an alternative to mechanical valves. These patients are more active than the typical elderly patient and have a lifestyle in which they are not willing to conform to the constraints of being chained to a blood thinner and its deleterious effects and constant lab results.

The facts as they stand at the time of this writing are as follows:

- TAVRS are only for the replacement of your aortic valve; the technology as of today is just in its infancy for trials of transcatheter mitral valve replacement. This has led to several medical device companies competing to bring transcatheter mitral valves to the medical marketplace.

- However, in 2013 the FDA cleared the first TMVR (Transcatheter Mitral Valve Repair) device, the

MitraClip. More than 40,000 patients have received the *MitraClip* with the post-procedural data very encouraging.

- TAVR can be used only if it is replacing your original valve or a prior bioprosthetic valve, called VIV TAVR, (Valve-in-Valve). **You cannot have a TAVR if you have a mechanical aortic valve in place.** Furthermore, every valve-in-valve procedure narrows the opening of the aortic valve with each subsequent placement. In other words, you cannot keep putting a straw inside a straw; eventually, the opening will become too narrow for fluid to flow through it.

- Originally TAVR was approved only for the *very sick*, those considered so fragile that they could not survive the traditional trans-sternal, cardiopulmonary bypass operation. Unfortunately, those patients were left to succumb to their cardiac disease. As the research progressed, TAVR was expanded to *high-surgical-risk* patients for open heart surgery. Such a patient could have had an open heart procedure but was at extreme risk for mortality failure. Studies are now under way to expand TAVRs to patients considered *low or intermediate surgical risks.*

- Following a TAVR procedure, patients are at an increased risk of needing a pacemaker. Depending on the type of TAVR valve placed (Edwards Sapien or Medtronic CoreValve), the need for a pacemaker intra or post-operatively can be as high as 20 percent. Add to this a pre-existing right/left bundle branch block (heart electrical conduction problems) and aortic calcium, and your chances of needing a pacemaker increase significantly. *This one factor alone may become the Achilles' heel of TAVR being viable in low-risk patient groups.*

- TAVR's high success rate of being statistically "non-inferior to surgery" applies only to the transfemoral approach TAVRs (the preferred approach to valve placement); transapical, subclavian, and trans-carotid approaches lack this accolade.

So now you can see the logic of some of these patients. They think:

Heck, 15 years from now TAVRs may be so perfected that transcatheter aortic valve replacement will be commonplace. I'll just get a bioprosthetic valve, stay off Coumadin and wait for the technology to catch up to me.

And they could be right; time will tell.

Jackie from *Facebook Surgery Open Heart* writes:

I had my aortic [valve] replaced almost 2 years ago and replaced with a cow valve (at age 50) ... I pray if I need mine replaced again they can use the TAVR or something minimally invasive! One of the risks I took in getting a bioprosthetic valve is that they don't last as long as mechanical, but I didn't want to take blood thinners. My Dad had a mechanical aortic valve inserted in 1989 (I was born with a bicuspid aortic valve like him) and he struggled with Coumadin... but after going through OHS [open heart surgery] I wasn't sure if maybe I made the wrong decision, because with a mechanical valve there would be less chance of going through that again. If they keep perfecting TAVR then if I need a replacement in the future maybe it will be an option. And that gives me hope!

Take note, however, that there are a multitude of other factors, from aortic size limitations to the shape of your heart that may not make you a viable candidate for a TAVR procedure 15 years from now — even if TAVR is eventually offered to all risk groups. Thus, if this is an avenue affecting your decision, you must have a *long talk* with your cardiologist and surgeon. ***Be sure your decision is an informed one based totally on your own medical circumstances as discussed with your doctor. Not every person is a candidate for TAVR surgery even if the option becomes available to all risk-group candidates!***

Won't it though, won't TAVR eventually be offered to all patients, in all risk categories?

If you ask *Edwards* and *Medtronic*, the two primary transcatheter valve companies, they would most likely say *yes*. As of this writing, three FDA approved studies are being examined: the *Partner 1, Partner 2 and Partner 3* trials. Each is studying transcatheter aortic valves in *high-risk, intermediate-risk* and *low-risk* patients, respectively. *Edwards* states that the preliminary report for its *Sapien 3 Valve* is in and its data is promising. Its news release and the data from the *Partner 2* trial demonstrate TAVR to be superior to surgery at one-year post-op on its primary endpoint of mortality, stroke, and moderate/severe aortic regurgitation.

The goal for TAVR has always been the above stated, become equal to if not superior to surgical aortic valve placement; once that goal has been achieved the next milestone is what doctors call *structural valve degeneration*. And although it has varying definitions, most doctors would agree that for most patients it is defined by *freedom from reoperation. How long will this new TAVR valve last before it starts to degenerate or fail?*

The first *Partner 1 Trial*, which studied 2400 patients, revealed that five years out from a TAVR procedure, structural valve deterioration was not frequently occurring. This showed that for the very sick, (those too fragile for a traditional open heart procedure), TAVR was the correct surgical option. These patients tended to be very old and quite ill (80 to 90 years of age) and if no intervention were to be performed, they would most likely succumb to their aortic valve disease. This was considered the *high surgical risk group*. However, as TAVR has now expanded and become approved for FDA trial for intermediate to low surgical risk groups, the question becomes: *What about past five years out?*

Remember, TAVRs were FDA approved in the United States only five years ago. Their modern infancy worldwide only dates back to around 2006. So, we are just starting to receive 10-year data on TAVR durability at a decade out.

What are the long-term results?

They are not as promising as the interventional world had hoped. Reported at the EuroPCR 2016: Among those patients who survived past five years, up to half saw their valves start to degenerate by 10 years post implantation. As stated earlier, for that high surgical risk octogenarian, this is of no concern. However, for the *low-risk* patient looking to TAVR as their primary valve replacement; or more germane to our conversation, as their secondary replacement of their first bioprosthetic valve 10 to 15 years later, the data is not as encouraging as one would hope. It should also be noted that this data did not take into consideration VIV (valve-in-valve) patients. This populace was excluded from the study. A person opting for an open heart bioprosthetic aortic valve in the hopes of a TAVR valve in the future would be considered a VIV patient. The

129

doctor would be placing a TAVR aortic valve into a previously placed bioprosthetic valve.

The pundits may argue (and perhaps rightfully so) that degeneration is not failure. And a good majority of these patients can survive years with a degenerative valve. They will also argue that most of these studies looked at first-generation TAVR valves. Newer generation valves, such as the *Edwards Sapien 3*, display far fewer paravalvular leaks, which could lead to less degeneration. This may all be true, and its fruition does seem eventually inevitable. However, for the subject presented in this chapter and as to our discussion of TAVR influencing mechanical versus bioprosthetic valve choices, all the information stated above and all the studies must be weighed before the patient makes an aortic valve decision. Don't be so quick to let potential future technology influence your decisions today. Talk to your doctor, your cardiologist, and even your surgeon; their opinions may vary, but in the end, you will have investigated all the possibilities and made an informed decision based on your personal preferences and the current data available today.

However, right here, right now, as of this writing, *open-heart surgery is the Gold Standard for treating aortic valve disease in low- to intermediate-risk patients*. Still, having said that, TAVR is gaining ground incrementally. As stated earlier, the latest statistics expounded by *Edwards* state that, statistically, TAVR is *"better than surgery for Intermediate-Risk patients."*

Touting information gleaned from the Partner II trial on intermediate-risk patients, Edwards states: *"Transcatheter aortic valve replacement (TAVR) with the Edwards SAPIEN 3 valve demonstrated 75 percent lower rates of 30-day all-cause mortality and disabling stroke compared to surgery in intermediate-risk patients."*

130

Appendix C: Atrial Fibrillation and Treatments

Atrial Fibrillation

Normally your heart beats in a nice, synchronous rhythm, easily moving blood from the upper chambers (the atria) to the lower chambers (the ventricles). When there is a disruption to these synchronous beats, it can be the result of *atrial fibrillation*. When atrial fibrillation occurs, the upper atria of your heart beat irregularly, *in fact, they quiver at about 300 to 600 times per minute;* a healthy atrium beats/contracts 60 to 80 times per minute.

Think about how your body is on a beautiful, warm day – all your movements are smooth and synchronized. Then picture yourself outside without a jacket on an extremely cold day – you immediately start to shiver. That shivering is exactly what your upper atria are doing in atrial fibrillation. Of course, it's not that your atria are cold— it's just a good analogy for how your heart is reacting during AFib.

Now, although you may feel fine (and some people may not even know they have AFib), atrial fibrillation is not benign. Patients with AFib are at an increased risk for stroke or a heart-related incident leading to death. *Up to 20 percent of people who have strokes have AFib.* The problem is that all this upper atria quivering causes blood to pool in the atrial chamber.

Have you ever walked along a stream and noticed that

although it is readily flowing, there are areas along the bank where the water swirls around, never flowing away? These are called eddy currents. If you watch closely, all the residue and film in that area collects and swirls along with the water. Eventually, some debris breaks free and rides along with the stream.

This is what happens in atrial fibrillation. The quivering within your upper atria causes blood to pool and swirl around in the atria. Unfortunately, when blood is not flowing, it tends to clot; these clots (just like the debris in the stream) eventually break loose and, depending on where they flow, can cause stroke, heart attack, or pulmonary (lung) emboli. For this reason, many patients with chronic atrial fibrillation are placed on blood thinners, mainly Coumadin.

Although people with atrial fibrillation can lead normal, healthy lives, it is not a benevolent heart syndrome. The ventricles of the heart depend on the reception of regular, consistent signals from the atria; *the atria and ventricles are meant to work in synchronous harmony.* In AFib, the rapid firings from the atria can cause the ventricles to beat 100 to 150 times a minute. Your normal heart rate should be around 60 to 100 beats per minute. All this can eventually lead to heart failure, a condition in which your heart can't pump enough blood to meet the body's requirements. AFib reduces your heart's pumping ability by 10 to 30 percent.

Atrial fibrillation usually presents in three distinct patterns: *paroxysmal, persistent,* and *permanent.* Although atrial fibrillation may start out somewhat benign, it is a progressive disease; if left untreated, over time it may advance and become much more severe. Also, untreated and prolonged AFib can create new pathways for electrical activity in the heart. It may start in the pulmonary vein area of the atria, but can easily expand to other regions of the heart; doctors call this *atrial remodeling.* Once remodeling has occurred, effective treatments such as ablations are less likely to offer relief. *The longer you have untreated AFib, the harder it is to reestablish a normal heart rhythm.*

In **paroxysmal**, the atrial fibrillation onsets spontaneously and then stops just as suddenly, usually within 24 hours to one week. The duration can be greater than 30 seconds and its catalyst or etiology can have several foundations, even simple factors such as stress, alcohol, medications or nicotine. Its incident increases with age and although it is normally not life-threatening, it can have serious consequences further down the road. Thus, diagnosing and seeking treatment as early as possible is crucial.

As stated above, AFib can result from many causes, ranging from a previous heart attack to smoking, extreme stress to something as minor as a lack of sleep or too much coffee. However, the most prevalent cause is existing heart disease or a recent heart surgery, especially heart valve surgery or coronary artery bypass.

Whatever the cause, AFib's symptoms can be frightening: fatigue, dizziness, shortness of breath, and a racing heart, to name just a few. If you are experiencing paroxysmal fibrillation, don't be lulled by its transient effects — its ability to quickly subside. Even if symptoms do go away, it is important to seek medical advice and have the proper tests performed, starting with an EKG.

Persistent atrial fibrillation is very similar to paroxysmal. The main difference is that persistent, as its name implies, continues for more than one week. Just as in paroxysmal, it may also resolve on its own, but usually needs medical/procedural intervention to cease.

Permanent atrial fibrillation's genesis may derive from paroxysmal and persistent AFib; however, no matter its etiology, it is a condition that does not spontaneously resolve on its own. It is also a disease process that most doctors are unwilling to tolerate in today's modern society. In other words, to be diagnosed with permanent atrial fibrillation means the patient and the doctor have decided not to try to restore the patient's heart to its normal sinus rhythm. Today there are so many options available for the treatment of AFib, from medications to interventional procedures, that the decision to not treat this process is becoming increasingly atypical. This is coupled with the fact that the longer one tolerates AFib, the harder it becomes to manage and resolve in the future — the remodeling we just talked about. *Atrial fibrillation endured for more than six months is already becoming resistant to treatment.*

Atrial Fibrillation Diagnosis

The first test usually given to diagnose AFib is a simple, non-invasive EKG (electrocardiogram). Here several leads are placed on your chest and your heart's electrical activity is recorded and analyzed. If your atrial fibrillation is permanent and consistent, it will be recorded at that very moment; however, if you have paroxysmal or persistent AFib, you may need to wear a device called a *Holter Monitor* for 24 to 48 hours. This monitor is portable and resembles a small purse; it will record your heart activity for a day or two. You may also be asked to wear an *Event Monitor*. This is very similar to the Holter Monitor; however, with this monitor, you push a button to record an event as you feel it happening. Your cardiologist or electrophysiologist can also surgically place an event monitor – called a *loop recorder* – under your skin. This tiny device, no bigger than a stick of gum, is surgically placed under your skin and records all your heart activity. Its placement is considered minor surgery.

Further testing can lead to a cardiac stress test, echo test or invasive electrophysiological study, in which your doctor purposely induces irregular beats and observes how your heart responds. A blood test will determine whether you have an electrolyte imbalance or thyroid hormone problem.

Atrial Fibrillation Risks: Stroke

Warfarin (Coumadin) patients reduce their stroke risk by 65 percent as compared to patients not on blood-thinning medication.

Know the signs of stroke:

- Numbness or weakness, particularly on one side of the body

- Drooping on one side of the face

- Trouble speaking, slurred speech, mild to severe confusion

- Dizziness, trouble walking or with balance

- Severe headache, trouble seeing in one or both eyes

If stroke is suspected, dial 911!

With the advent of a powerful blood-thinning drug called tPA (Tissue Plasminogen Activator), emergency doctors talk about the *golden three-hour window* to survive a stroke. This is the period of time following a stroke during which doctors feel it is safe to use tPA (which is a very successful medication in the treatment of strokes).

Any time after this window, it is considered too risky to use this medication therapy. The point is no matter what treatment is to come, it is imperative to seek help immediately when a stroke is suspected. Every minute delayed is a lost opportunity for a full recovery.

Atrial Fibrillation Treatments

Medications are usually the first treatments offered for atrial fibrillation. Coumadin and other blood thinners are often given first to prevent the clot formation we spoke about earlier. If the AFib doesn't resolve on its own (paroxysmal or persistent), the patient may be given rate control medications to try to slow the heartbeat. These drugs (usually beta blockers, calcium channel blockers or cardiac glycoside) all slow the heart rate and relax the blood vessels. These medications work on the heart's AV (atrioventricular) node and can slow the heart rate to below 100 beats by blocking the extra atrial signals from reaching the heart's ventricles. Electrical signals coming from the atria must pass through this node to reach the ventricles. This is not dissimilar to the electricity that must pass through a light switch to reach a light bulb. Replace a standard light switch with a dimmer switch and suddenly you have greater control over the amount of electricity that can affect the bulb.

If the rate medication is ineffective, your doctor may offer the more precarious rhythm control drugs; he may refer to this as chemical or pharmacologic cardioversion. These medications have more severe side effects and necessitate closer cardiac monitoring. The most effective of these drugs, Amiodarone, is usually used as a last resort due to its toxicity to the lungs.

Several invasive procedures can be used to restore your heart to its normal rhythm.

- Electrical Cardioversion: electrode pads are placed on your chest and low energy shocks are applied to try to convert your heart back to its normal rhythm. Don't worry; you are sedated prior to the application of these shocks and they are not the great big shocks seen on medical television shows in which the body leaps off the table with each jolt. Weeks before the cardioversion, your doctor may place you on blood thinners to prevent any blood clots in your atria from breaking free during your cardioversion and causing a stroke.

137

- Catheter Ablation: here, an electrophysiologist places a small wire through a vein in your leg or arm (just like a cardiac angioplasty) and threads it up to your heart. Energy waves are then used to precisely disrupt the area in your atria that is firing random signals. This catheter uses either radio waves, cryotherapy (extreme cold) or laser waves to create scar tissue that blocks signals from traveling to unwanted areas of the heart. Prior to an ablation, your doctor will perform an electrical mapping of your heart. By placing an electrical catheter in your heart, he/she can determine the exact locations of the electrical activity. He/she will then use the map to accurately ablate the problem areas and hopefully restore your heart to its normal rhythm. However, sometimes atrial fibrillation may return and the ablation procedure may need to be repeated at some point in the future.

- Maze Procedure: this procedure requires open-heart surgery. Here your surgeon makes small cuts, burns, or cryo-freezes that scar areas of the atria, preventing the aberrant electrical signals from crossing the scarred areas. This procedure is also the reason for and the focus of the above-stated discourse on atrial arrhythmias since the Maze procedure is an open-heart procedure and the focus of this book.

Maze Surgical Ablation

Most maze procedures (up to 90 percent) are performed as a secondary or concomitant procedure; this means most patients need open-heart surgery bypasses or valve replacement and the cardiac ablation is secondary to their primary surgery.

It would be extremely rare for a patient to have a cardio-pulmonary open-heart procedure just for a maze ablation.

If it is performed as the primary procedure, usually a sternotomy is not the main approach. Your surgeon will most likely perform a closed chest procedure like a *mini maze* or a *minimally invasive maze*. Minimally invasive maze surgery can be either robotic-assisted or performed using a thoracoscopic (the side of your chest) approach. This minimally invasive surgery eliminates the need to divide your sternum, place you on a cardio-pulmonary bypass machine, and stop your heart.

During this open-heart procedure, the patient is placed on a heart-lung machine and the heart is stopped, allowing the surgeon to open it. *Remember in our earlier chapter we discussed how to replace your heart valves, the heart must be entered; it is the same situation here.* To place the ablating maze probe, your surgeon must open your heart.

Your surgeon uses either radio waves, microwaves, ultrasound, cryolesions, or small incisions to create scar tissue in the left and right atria. Scar tissue does not conduct electricity and, thus, disrupts the erratic paths of electrical impulses; it also prevents random electrical signals from recurring. The signals from the atria can then once again conduct through a controlled pathway (a maze) to the lower ventricles, restoring a normal heart rhythm. The atrium is then sewn back together to be once again functional.

A maze procedure has favorable statistical long-term results; up to 90 percent of patients receiving a maze see an end to their atrial fibrillation. However, do beware; this may not mean you will be able to cease your rhythm or rate medications altogether.

Doug from a cardiac *Facebook* forum writes:

Good morning to all, I wanted to share an update. I had been on and off AFib for 15 years. I went through atenolol, metoprolol, sotalol. None really worked. Toward the end, I was in AFib about 40 percent of the time.

I had a cryoablation on December 29th. It was for me a very easy, painless process. I have now been AFib free for over ten weeks. I went off sotalol three weeks ago, no issues. I will be going off Xeralto in a couple weeks.

Not only do I feel so much better, but my energy level is amazing. I have more drive and mental focus than I have had in those 15 years of AFib. I am sharing this as hope and encouragement. I don't plan to disappear from this site as I want to help others as I was helped.

What is the difference between a cardiologist and an electrophysiologist?

When someone begins to experience heart troubles, he or she is usually sent to a cardiologist: a specialist in heart abnormalities. If further testing reveals the heart ailment is an arrhythmia or a problem with the heart's electrical system, that person is sent to an electrophysiologist.

Electrophysiology is a cardiac sub-specialty that focuses on testing and treating the arrhythmias of the heart. Your electrophysiologist (or EP specialist) is a cardiologist MD who has gone an extra one to two years to become this specialist. *When you do the math, it is an incredible amount of education: four years of college (premed), four years of medical school, three years of internal medicine training, three years to become a cardiologist, and one to two more years to become an electrophysiologist!*

Your EP has the skill and ability to perform procedures such as percutaneous catheter ablations, pacemaker insertions, and AICD (cardiac defibrillator) insertions. However, an EP is not a surgeon. He/she cannot perform open-heart surgery or maze procedures. On the other hand, a cardiac surgeon is sanctioned and does have the skills to perform maze procedures, pacemakers and AICD implantations, and, of course, open-heart surgery.

Appendix D: Heart Bypass Surgery vs. PCI Stenting

If you are reading this section, most likely you have been told you have some level of cardiovascular heart disease. For most people, this manifests in the form of needing either open heart bypass surgery, cardiac balloon angioplasty and stenting, or regimens of cardiac medications.

If open heart surgery is your recommended route, then this usually entails needing anywhere between one and five bypasses via a cardiac surgeon. If it is angioplasty and stenting then most likely you have one to three arteries that must be repaired, and you will be seeing an interventional cardiologist. If you and your cardiologist decide on the most conservative route, you will be placed on medications to control your cardiac disease and possible bouts of angina. Of course, the big question that arises is:

How do I choose between heart bypass surgery, cardiac stenting, or medication therapy?

For most patients, there really is no choice.

If you are having a heart attack and are rushed to the hospital, then an emergency procedure of either bypass or angioplasty is going to be a quick and decisive course of action. Most patients, when presented in these situations, are most likely going to urgently take the suggestion of their doctor and be rushed into the intervention that is recommended.

For other, less-urgent situations (patients with stable coronary artery disease), the severity of the blockage(s) and their locations on your heart will determine the most appropriate interventional route. Your overall physical health will also be factored.

Not all blockages are amenable to angioplasty and stenting. Nor can medication solve all problems. Sometimes open heart surgery is the only avenue available to keep you safe and alive. This is why it is so important to find a cardiologist you have come to trust and rely on. In most circumstances, it will be his/her recommendation that will influence, if not dictate, your choice of interventions.

Women are from Venus

Heart attack! We've all seen it in the movies and on TV. The man grabs his chest with both hands, makes some primordial sound, then falls to one knee, and finally collapses on the ground.

The sign is as familiar as the "I am choking" neck grip.

But wait a minute. Why is it always the man we see on TV? What about the women? I never see them displaying the same dramatic scene when they are depicting a heart attack. *There may be a reason for that!*

Many women who have a heart attack never experience pain; if they do, it can start out as just mild pain and discomfort and it can be in several places other than their chest. Some women stated that prior to their heart attack they felt pain in their upper abdomen, jaw, back, neck, and sometimes even shoulder. They can experience dizziness, lightheadedness, sweating, shortness of breath, and extreme fatigue.

However, no matter what the symptoms and how severe the pain, the biggest problem for women is their readiness to accept the fact that they may be having a heart attack. Couple this with a strong devotion to family and tasks — *I heard a story where the woman definitely suspected she was having a heart attack, but she needed to pick up the kids from school first* — and you have a situation that can be perilous, if not deadly. According to a 2016 report from the American Heart Association, a heart attack strikes someone every 43 seconds!

Cathy from *Surgery Open Heart* Facebook writes about her heart attack:

I didn't know what was happening to me. I mean, you see people on TV and what happens. So that wasn't like mine at all. I got the pain down my right arm and mild chest pains but nothing really bad. And I got, like, a lump in my throat. So I had no clue it could be my heart.

PCI Angioplasty (Percutaneous Coronary Intervention) vs. Heart Bypass Surgery

Since the advent of cardiac stenting, there has been a medical controversy between bypass surgery and stents. *Which is the better alternative? Do patients with coronary artery disease fare better with bypass surgery or stenting?*

Despite all the countless studies, the controversy remains unsettled. Add to the mix current medication therapy and you find yourself in a trifecta of confusion.

The confusion arises mainly from the baseline measuring point one decides to use:

- *Are we measuring procedure vs. recovery time?*

  If so, medication and stenting become clear winners. An angioplasty and stenting can be done under local anesthesia with a small cut in your groin or wrist. Your hospital stay can be one or two days and your recovery very quick. Open heart surgery, on the other hand, requires days to a week in the hospital, general anesthesia, and a prolonged recovery period.

- *What is the most durable procedure; what offers the longest survival rate?*

  Most surgeons will state bypass surgery is still the *Gold Standard* for life longevity, especially in the presence of complex coronary artery disease. However, some studies challenge these standards, stating that new second-generation drug eluting stents are becoming very competitive.

- *How many arteries are blocked, how severe is the blockage, and where are they located?*

If it is a single or double coronary artery with low-risk narrowing, angioplasty may be the answer. Conversely, if your coronary artery is too small or completely blocked, angioplasty may not be possible. If it is multi-vessel disease, with your main heart artery (LAD) very narrowed, your cardiologist may recommend bypasses. However, once again, some cardiologists are very comfortable stenting multi-vessel heart disease, along with your LAD, which supplies 60 to 70 percent of the heart's myocardium (the muscle tissue of the heart).

Some cardiologist will also offer to stent your Left Main Coronary Artery, also referred to as the Left Coronary Artery. Some patients may get this confused with the LAD (Left Anterior Descending Artery). The Left Main Coronary Artery is a segment of artery before your LAD that supplies up to 70 percent of the blood to the myocardium of the heart. This small section of artery is considered the most important artery in the human body. Remember, this one small segment supplies up to 70 percent of your heart's blood supply. Get arterial stenosis to this area and it is like narrowing the main water supply pipe going from the street to your home. You could get by with the faucet in the bathroom or the kitchen slowing to a drip, but clog up the main supply pipe to your house and it becomes catastrophic.

LAD Artery (Your Most Important Artery)

The LAD artery gets its notorious label as the "Widow Maker" for good reason. This one artery, along with its branches, supplies most of the blood to the left ventricle of your heart. Have a major blockage to this artery and your chances of survival are minimal.

Along with supplying a vast portion of your heart's blood supply, the LAD is also the major blood supplier to the bundle branches of the heart's conduction system – the electrical currents that beat your heart. Blockage of this area of your heart can cause what doctors call bundle branch block and a certain heart attack.

- *How is the patient's overall health?*

Are there other co-morbidities that must be taken into consideration? Some patients are so frail that open heart surgery just isn't possible; in that case, stenting or medication is the most logical route. Just having diabetes alone may mean bypass surgery is the better path. Add left anterior descending artery (your most important heart artery), diabetes, heart failure, and significant narrowing of your vessels – most, if not all, cardiologists would most likely recommend bypass surgery.

- *Does the patient present with Acute Coronary Syndrome?*

Acute coronary syndrome means that the patient has either unstable angina or an MI (Myocardial Infarction). In these situations, the cardiologist may suggest stenting over bypass surgery, especially if only one or two vessel disease is present.

- *Does the patient wish to have a procedure that may offer a permanent resolution or is he/she willing to have multiple smaller procedures?*

  Restenosis is a limitation that comes with angioplasty and stenting. This is not to suggest that heart bypass grafts also don't become narrowed over time; however, some studies show that stents can have up to a 10-percent chance of restenosis (becoming a blocked artery again). If you look on some of the heart forums, some patients claim to have had more than 10 to 15 stent procedures in their lifetime. It is not unusual for a patient who has undergone stenting or angioplasty to need a follow-up procedure within the next four years.

Every patient and every situation will be different. That is why a clear and concise conversation must take place with your cardiologist. Don't be afraid to ask the questions and concerns on your mind. Write them down before your next appointment. When you are first told that you need some type of cardiac procedure, your mind will most likely cloud over and you may not even hear or digest what your doctor is telling you. If time allows, go home and absorb what he has said, then come back prepared to understand what your options may be.

It is when you are offered time and avenues that these dilemmas become choices. Your cardiologist is going to tell you how many blockages you have, how severe they are, and where they are located on your heart. All these factors, along with your health, age, and life circumstances are going to guide your doctor in terms of what he recommends as the best options for you. If time permits, as stated earlier, he may allow you to go home and consider the options presented. If he does, or even in your first conversations, here are some keys questions you may want to ask:

1. Is this something that needs to be addressed immediately?

2. Did I have or am I having a heart attack, and if so, was there any damage to my heart muscles?

3. Is the angina I am experiencing stable or unstable? (Have him/her explain the difference to you.)

4. Out of the three options available – bypass surgery, angioplasty, or medication – which is the best for my circumstances?

5. Which options offered to me will require me to be placed on a blood thinner (dual antiplatelet therapy) like aspirin, Plavix, or Coumadin? How long will how have to take it and how will that affect my quality of life?

Don't be afraid to ask your cardiologist about clinical trials. Much of today's procedures are predicated on their results. The more recent BEST Trail espouses that for patients with multi-vessel coronary artery disease, heart bypass surgery displayed fewer adverse events than PCI-stenting *even with* modern drug-eluding stents. These findings echoed previous studies that espoused the same clinical outcomes: *heart bypass surgery yielded better results in patients with multi-vessel heart disease even when compared to second-generation drug-eluding stents.*

And although the BEST Trial was terminated due to slow enrollment, in long-term follow-ups the PCI group had more spontaneous MI's and needed more repeat revascularizations than patients having open heart bypass surgery. In contrast, heart bypass patients presented with a higher risk of stroke postoperatively compared to the PCI patients.

However, don't be swayed so easily. The PRECOMBAT study randomized 600 adult patients in Korea to have either PCI drug-eluding stenting or CABG. The groups were split evenly, with about 70 percent of the patients having left main artery stenosis along with two to three other vessels diseased. At five years out, most patients were on aspirin as a blood-thinning regimen and about 50 percent were receiving beta blockers alone or along with a statin drug. On average, the PCI patients received about three stents and the CABG patients had the equivalent of around three bypasses. At the five-year mark, there was no significant difference between the two groups in terms of what clinicians called *primary end points*. Primary end points (or MACCE end points) looked at a composite of death from any cause: stroke, MI, or repeat percutaneous or surgical revascularization for newly formed lesions.

All in all, stent technology is on a fast-paced track of development. Stents originally started in 1986 as a small plain lattice metal structure that held open your coronary artery; then science realized that if coated with certain medications (drug eluding), these same stents could stay open longer and fight off neointimal hyperplasia (restenosis from the growth of scar tissue within the stent).

However, when all is said and done, the above statements are just an inkling of a long and complicated study. **Don't take the offered brief synopsis as a concrete decision stone.** Talk to your cardiologist and ask him/her about studies like the BEST, EXCEL, and SYNTAX trials. It can lead to great discussions on what you are being offered and how statistically it is perceived in today's modern medicinal world.

Although the ultimate decision falls to you the patient, in most cases it should be a collaborative effort between your cardiologist, the interventional cardiologist, and your cardiac surgeon. Patients who are approached by a *heart team* statistically have better results and outcomes than do those offered just one viewpoint from only one practitioner. A good cardiologist will not only provide this team but will also offer what is called a *"shared decision-making process."* This is a collaborative process in which the patient and the doctor work in unison to reach the best healthcare decision together; taking into account clinical data, best modern practices, and, most importantly, the patient's values and preferences.

PCI Stenting vs. Medical Therapy

When you have coronary artery disease, the arteries that supply blood to your heart muscle become clogged by plaque. This plaque and the subsequent blood clots that may form can reduce, if not totally occlude (block completely), the blood flow to your heart muscle. The resulting pain from this disease process is called *angina*. This lack of blood flow, along with its vital oxygen, is called *ischemia*. If the lack of blood flow is to the heart, it is called *cardiac ischemia*.

Doctors label angina as either *stable* or *unstable*. If your angina is stable, it occurs with a usual pattern of frequency and onset. **Stable angina is the only type of angina that falls under the above-stated heading of *Stenting versus Medical Therapy*.** (If you are having *unstable angina*, it is usually a medical emergency and your choices are narrowed and emergent.)

Your options for either are going to be governed by your medical history, your other health issues, your age, the

151

severity of your heart disease, and, of course, your personal desires.

> Unstable angina presents as a change in its occurrences, pattern, duration, and severity. It is *usually* associated with a heart attack or MI (*myocardial infarction*). Its occurrence can at times damage part of your heart muscle. If this has happened, you have experienced what doctors call *acute coronary syndrome*. This condition is an emergency and the patient needs to be taken to a hospital immediately. Studies clearly show that cardiac stenting in these situations reduces the rate of death in patients and subsequent escalation of their myocardial ischemia.

Several factors determine whether medical therapy or cardiac angioplasty is warranted. The results of your tests and studies will most likely be the greatest determinate. However, many cardiologists will recommend medical therapy initially unless you have underlying circumstances that require a more aggressive route. These conditions are usually related to patients who, despite aggressive medical therapy, still have persistent and debilitating symptoms, as well as patients whose studies show that they are at "high risk" for a severe heart attack.

Have a long discussion with your doctor; most studies show that medical therapy (along with lifestyle changes) has about the same results in preventing heart attacks and life longevity in patients with **stable** angina. These same studies go on to show that for some patients, angioplasty does not lower their risk of heart attacks over the medical therapy route. However, angioplasty may be more advantageous in the case of angina that is not relieved by medications, thus offering patients a more active lifestyle.

Angioplasty, however, is not without risks. Heart attacks and stroke, though rare, are still morbidities your doctor should go over with you. You may find that your doctor, depending on your findings, will suggest medical therapy first and angioplasty later if your symptoms do not abate. If you and your doctor decide on the more conservative route of medical treatment, you will most likely be placed on anti-anginal medication.

So, what is one to do?

You are diagnosed with stable coronary artery disease, and your physician offers you the choice of medical therapy or cardiac stenting – or both. Ask your doctor the question. However, most studies indicate that there is no difference between PCI and medical therapy in nonfatal heart attack patients. In other words, there is no clear indication of choosing one treatment over another in patients with stable coronary artery angina. Thus, patients who fall into this subset must be determined individually according to their clinical presentation, heart ischemia anatomy, and co-morbidities.

Where the studies become confusing is when you look at what outcomes are most important to you. The 2007 COURAGE trial revealed that patients with stable coronary artery disease had improved symptom control if they had PCI plus OMT (optimal medical therapy) versus if they had just medical therapy alone. So, if you are talking symptom relief, the evidence of this study is clear; both therapies together are the best option. However, if you and your physician are looking at this study in terms of myocardial infarction and (forgive me) death, this study showed no difference in the two treatment groups. Simply stated, this study showed that if you are having cardiac symptoms that are compromising or threatening your life, PCI is well justified. However, patients without quality-of-life-limiting symptoms may do just as well with OMT and no stenting, with stenting being an option further down the road in what some physicians refer to as a *wait-and-see* medical strategy.

The studies vary, and each person interprets the venues in different ways. However, the primary goal for you, the patient, should always be the same. The goals of therapy, whether CABG, PCI, or OMT, in patients with stable ischemic heart disease, should be to minimize symptoms, slow down coronary artery disease, and prevent possible future heart attacks (MI's).

Medication Compliance

No matter which intervention you receive (CABG, PCI, OMT); all have a high level of failure if you do not adhere to the medication therapy prescribed to you after your procedure. Recent studies have shown that patients who were strictly compliant with their prescribed medications fared far better than non-compliant patients when it came to what doctors refer to as a *MACE* (Major Adverse Cardiac Events). These events would be a measure of the safety and effectiveness of interventional treatments received as measured by heart attacks, strokes, or the need for revascularization of a previous intervention.

The medications typically prescribed after most procedures are the antiplatelet drugs, such as aspirin, Plavix, Brilinta, and Aggrenox. Also, most patients are placed on statins for cholesterol control and beta blockers to protect the heart.

These same studies showed that patients who tended to be "non-compliant" with their medications did far better with CABG's rather than PCI interventions. This was probably due to the fact that most patients with cardiac stents needed a higher level of antiplatelet medications than those who had just cardiac bypass grafts. The reasons for non-compliance vary in studies and real-world observations; however, education, language, finances, and marital status all seem to be factors.

So, what does this all mean in layman's terms?

As Shakespeare once said: *To thine own self be true...* If you believe you are one of those patients who will most likely not be compliant with the medication regimens prescribed to you, talk to your doctor about this. It may be a hard thing to admit, but if your baseline personality is such, then other cardiac interventions may be a better choice for you. Certainly, for those facing the choice between CABG and PCI, for the non-compliant patient, CABG may be a better long-term solution. Your doctor is well aware of non-compliant behaviors and will surely take that into consideration when offering you cardiac interventional avenues.

Appendix E: ASD/VSD (Congenital Septal Defects)

When I was about 15 years old, I remember hearing that my cousin had a hole in his heart about the size of a quarter. I had enough knowledge back then to surmise that no one could live with a hole in his heart. All the blood would leak out and the person; my cousin would bleed to death long before the hole was discovered!

Of course, I now know that the hole was not on the outer tissue of the heart but was rather a hole in the septum that divides the ventricles or the atriums. Atrial and ventricular septal defects are both congenital abnormalities in the membrane of the heart that separates the right side of the heart from the left side. If the concept is still confusing, remember that you have a nasal septum; it is the tissue (cartilage and thin bone) that separates your right nostril from your left nostril. This septum, (just like the septum in your heart) separates the two nostrils so there is no mixing of air from each nostril – just as the septum of your heart separates oxygenated blood from de-oxygenated blood. And just as a hole can form in your heart septum, a hole or perforation can form between your two nostrils. The most common way this happens today is a nose piercing that rings from one nostril to the other. *Yuck! But I'm not judging!* Other ways are from long-term topical drug application, decongestion nasal spray abuse or prolonged cocaine snorting. Once the hole is formed in the nasal passage, air can flow from one side to the other (usually making a whistling sound). It is the same with the heart, where blood will flow from the left side to the right side.

No whistling sound, but a definite whooshing sound heard by stethoscope and called a murmur.

VSD (Ventricular Heart Defect)

As stated earlier, VSD is a hole in the wall inside your heart that separates the two lower chambers of your heart, called the ventricles. Communication is needed between the two chambers during development in the womb; however, once an infant is born, or actually before birth, this communication (opening) between the two chambers closes. Once closed, there is no longer the mixing of right-sided oxygen-poor blood with left-sided oxygen-rich blood. It is when this hole fails to close that the patient is born with VSD, ventricular septal defect. This defect changes the normal blood flow through the heart.

VSD is the most common congenital heart defect found in newborns, occurring in approximately one of every 500 births; it is also the most common congenital defect in adults, second only to bicuspid aortic valves. If the hole is small enough, it will not cause any undue strain on the heart and may close on its own. If the opening is too large to close on its own, its presence will allow blood from the left side of the heart to shunt over to the right side of the heart. This extra blood must then be pumped up to the lungs once again. All this extra re-pumped blood will make the heart and lungs work harder, and the lungs have the potential to become congested.

It's like being on a small boat that springs a leak. You start to bail the incoming water with a bucket, but every time you toss out the water, that same water comes back in the boat through your hole. If the hole is small enough, you can ignore it and easily row back to shore. If the hole is larger, it takes an enormous amount of effort to constantly toss it out of the boat over and over. This is what your heart

157

experiences when its right ventricle must pump out the blood it has already pumped out to the lungs. For this reason, most VSDs are surgically closed in children when they are very young, usually in the first few months of life.

In adult VSD, if the hole is small (less than 0.5 square centimeters), it may present as a heart murmur heard on the stethoscope. (Large VSDs are rare in adults in that they usually exhibit severe symptoms early and are repaired long before the child reaches puberty.) The small VSD (sometimes called *maladie de Roger)* can often exist without causing any undue strain on the patient; the opening is so small that the heart does not have to do any extra work to accommodate its abnormality.

You may hear your doctor mention *"ventricular volume overload or pulmonary hypertension."* He is referring to all that extra shunted blood your heart must pump and the injury it is causing the arteries supplying your lungs (pulmonary hypertension). Small or restrictive VSDs cause minuscule left-to-right shunting of blood; thus, *overload* of the left ventricle and *pulmonary hypertension* usually are not present. Moderate-sized septal defects display more shunting of blood, and the disease process acts accordingly – mild to moderate hypertension and overload beginning.

If the opening is larger and unrepaired in the adult, then symptoms are usually dependent on the size of the opening, its location in the septum, and the patient's other health co-morbidities. As a result of the heart having to pump harder, patients with adult VSD may experience pulmonary hypertension. This can present as shortness of breath, fatigue, and a profound overall weakness. If left untreated, a medium to large VSD can also cause heart failure, irregular heartbeats, and even stroke.

When a small to medium VSD becomes a problem, then surgical intervention is warranted. These problems present as high pulmonary pressures (pulmonary hypertension) and persistent endocarditis – inflammation of the lining of the heart.

Hallec, a forum member of *Surgery Open Heart Facebook*, writes:

I have an ASD and VSD that they will be closing and I have had these since birth. The reason I am having surgery is because I have gotten endocarditis twice in a lifetime which is very very rare! The last time was the beginning of the year [which] took a very hard toll on my body.

Endocarditis and Prophylactic Antibiotics

If you have a heart anomaly such as VSD or ASD, you are susceptible to what doctors call endocarditis. This is an infection of the heart lining and the heart's valves. This infection has the potential to become life-altering, if not life-threatening.

Endocarditis occurs when bacteria and germs in other parts of your body, via your bloodstream, travel to the compromised areas of your heart. There are several routes through which bacteria can enter the blood stream: skin infections, urinary tract infections, pneumonia, and even inflammatory bowel disease; however, one of the most common ways is through dental procedures. Your mouth is full of bacteria and germs; while getting a cleaning or dental procedure, the bacteria from your mouth can enter your blood stream and attach to the damaged areas of your heart. The propensity for this occurrence is highest primarily among those individuals with compromised heart valves, artificial heart valves, or, as stated, cardiac issues such as VSDs. It is rare to find endocarditis occurring in people without any heart abnormalities.

Endocarditis is usually treated with antibiotics and, on the extreme end, surgery and possible heart valve replacements. Most doctors and dentists will pre-treat patients with heart abnormalities with prophylactic (preventative) antibiotics prior to any dental procedure or cleaning. If you have a VSD, ASD (repaired or un-repaired), heart valve replacement or abnormality, or history of rheumatic fever, be sure to talk to your doctor about taking antibiotics before any mouth, throat, or tooth procedure. In 2007, the American Heart Association changed its recommendation for pre-treatment of antibiotics prior to certain procedures, so be sure to check with your dentist or doctor before taking any prophylactic medications. Some doctors will also recommend antibiotics for patients who have artificial patches in the upper portion of their bodies; an example of this would be a carotid patch after carotid endarterectomy surgery.

VSD Closures

Spontaneous closure of VSD, by some statistics, occurs in up to 60 percent in patients, usually during early childhood. However, some documented closures have occurred in patients in their teens to early forties. When closure does not occur and the patient becomes symptomatic from the defect, then surgical intervention is usually the option.

Most ventricular defects are closed via median sternotomy – open heart surgery. The patient is placed on the cardiopulmonary machine and his/her heart is opened. The surgeon closes the defect either directly by suturing or places a patch over the defect and sews it in place. Patch material can be a piece of the patient's own pericardium or a synthetic material, either Dacron or Gore-Tex.

Other, less-invasive devices can close the ventricular defect percutaneously through a groin stick. This procedure can be done under local anesthesia without having to enter the patient through a sternotomy. However, do take heed that there have been cases of *cardiac erosion* related to some of the devices on today's market. These erosion events can be life-threatening, so be sure to ask your cardiac interventionist about such devices and studies before opting for this non-invasive approach to closing your defect.

If you have a VSD or ASD, most doctors recommend careful follow-ups and monitoring; at minimum an echocardiogram at least every 2-3 years. You may be asymptomatic (no ill effects from your septal defect). However, as you age, you are at risk for endocarditis, arrhythmias, or aortic regurgitation.

ASD (Atrial Septal Defect)

Where VSD is the most common congenital heart defect found in newborns, atrial septal defect is one of the most common congenital heart defects found in adults—

161

approximately 1.6 per 1000 births. There are many different types of ASD, with the most common type being *secundum ASD*, a defect that opens in the middle of the atrial septum. About eight out of every 10 babies born with an ASD has a secundum defect. However, at least half of these secundum defects are small enough that they close on their own.

An ASD defect allows your oxygen-rich blood to shunt into the oxygen-poor chamber of your heart. Just as in VSD, the amount of blood shunting is directly linked to the size of the hole. If the opening is small, then most patients can expect a normal life function because the small hole does not tax the heart. However, late in life – around the age of 30 – a patient's left atrial pressure increases (usually because of ventricular and diastolic dysfunction) and if the opening is large enough, right heart enlargement occurs. The once healthy and active patient may start to exhibit fatigue and exercise intolerance. These cascading events can eventually lead to atrial fibrillation, SVTs (supraventricular tachycardia) and pulmonary hypertension. If left untreated or corrected, it can lead to a condition called *Eisenmenger's syndrome.*

Although Eisenmenger's syndrome is discussed in this ASD section, it should be noted that statistically, Eisenmenger's syndrome occurs in about 10 percent of ASD patients compared to 50 percent of VSD patients. Further, it is the size of the defect and the volume of the extra blood flowing to the lungs that directly contributes to the disease process.

Eisenmenger Syndrome (Rare and Late Onset)

When a patient has an opening in their septum, the normal shunting that occurs is from the high-pressure left side of the heart to the low-pressure right side of the heart. This shunting causes increased blood flow to the lungs, overtaxing both the heart and the lungs for years if uncorrected. Eventually, pulmonary hypertension sets in and the right side of the heart becomes the new high-pressure region. Now that the pressures have reversed and the right side of the heart is the high-pressure chamber, blood will naturally shunt from the high-pressure right side to the lower pressure left side of the heart. *(Confusing? Yeah, I'm the one writing it and I'm getting dizzy!)*

Now the blood that would normally be heading to the lungs to become rich in oxygen to send off to the rest of your body is shooting over to the left side of the heart (no oxygen on board) and being pumped to your body's tissues. Now all your tissues are expecting this oxygen-rich blood, but they are quickly disappointed. If left uncorrected for too long, the increased pressure in the lungs will start to cause irreversible damage to the lungs' blood vessels, called *pulmonary vascular obstructive disease*. If this occurs to the extreme, the patient may eventually need a heart and lung transplant.

Symptoms of Eisenmenger's are cyanotic-looking skin (pale grayish skin color), finger clubbing (heavy, rounded fingernails), dyspnea (shortness of breath), syncope (fainting spells), fatigue, and chest pain, to name just a few.

ASD Closure

The presence of symptoms (directly related or incidental) is why most adult ASD patients become surgical candidates for closure. Repetitive endocarditis, pulmonary hypotension, ventricular hypertrophy, and the desire for pregnancy are all reason for surgical interventions. However, surgical intervention can be controversial –

asymptomatic or low-symptomatic patients with small defects weighed against the risks of open heart surgery can make the decision contentious. Some surgeons and studies suggest that ASD closure, small or otherwise, should be closed before the age of 30, well before natural age-related heart conditions amplify a patient's ASD. In an often-cited study, closure of an ASD before the age of 25 showed patients had normal survival rates; however, patients that had their ASD closed after the age of 40 experienced increased mortality.

As with the VSD closure, either open heart surgery or a transcatheter closure device is the primary vehicle for septal closure. Transcatheter ASD closure is becoming more commonplace and the preferred methodology of closure as companies offer increasingly more sophisticated and easily deployed septal closure devices. Post-procedure be prepared to be on a prophylactic antibiotic for about 6 months to dissuade endocarditis as well as an antiplatelet drug such as aspirin.

Catheterization repair, much like cardiac stenting, involves a small catheter inserted into a vein in your arm, groin, or neck. It is then threaded into your heart and a small umbrella-type device is used to close the defect in your septum. Your heart's tissue will eventually grow over the closure device and incorporate it into its own matrix.

Beware, though; there has been controversy over some of the devices used. There have been incidents in which some devices caused tissue erosion inside the heart. These erosions can result in a life-threatening emergency. Talk to your doctor if this is a path you have chosen for repair.

ACHA (Adult Congenital Heart Association)

If you have a congenital heart defect the ACHA recommends that you be seen in an ACHD (Adult Congenital Heart Disease) center at least once; they also state the more complex your heart defect the more crucial your involvement with these specialized centers should be.

The ACHA mission is: *"To improve and extend the lives of the millions born with heart defects through education, advocacy, and the promotion of research."*

Within these ACHD centers all the staff (cardiologists, nurses, imaging technicians) have advanced expertise in evaluating and treating patients with ACHD. Take a look at their website; they are the leading experts and advocates for patients with congenital heart defects and they list all the ACHD centers in the United States and Canada.

www.achaheart.org

Made in the USA
Middletown, DE
04 October 2020